Step Forward
Language for Everyday Life

Workbook

SERIES DIRECTOR
Jayme Adelson-Goldstein

2 Renata Russo

OXFORD
UNIVERSITY PRESS

OXFORD
UNIVERSITY PRESS

198 Madison Avenue
New York, NY 10016 USA

Great Clarendon Street, Oxford OX2 6DP UK

Oxford University Press is a department of the University of Oxford.
It furthers the University's objective of excellence in research, scholarship,
and education by publishing worldwide in

Oxford New York

Auckland Cape Town Dar es Salaam Hong Kong Karachi
Kuala Lumpur Madrid Melbourne Mexico City Nairobi
New Delhi Shanghai Taipei Toronto

With offices in

Argentina Austria Brazil Chile Czech Republic France Greece
Guatemala Hungary Italy Japan Poland Portugal Singapore
South Korea Switzerland Thailand Turkey Ukraine Vietnam

OXFORD and OXFORD ENGLISH are registered trademarks of
Oxford University Press

Executive Publisher: Janet Aitchison
Editorial Manager: Stephanie Karras
Associate Editor: Ashli Caudle Totty
Art Director: Maj-Britt Hagsted
Senior Art Editor: Judi DeSouter
Production Manager: Shanta Persaud
Production Controller: Eve Wong

ISBN : 978 0 19 4392334

Printed in China
20 19

This book is printed on paper from certified and well- managed sources.

Illustrations: Kevin Brown/Top Dog Studios: 9, 16, 36, 38, 43, 44, 47, 48, 67, 78, 82;
Susan Spellman: 2, 4, 30, 34, 54, 56, 61, 69, 79; Karen Minot: 12, 13, 21, 22, 27,
37, 41, 42, 45, 49, 50, 55, 56, 58, 70, 77, 84; Shawn Banner: 33, 52, 73, 77; Laurie
A. Conley: 6, 18, 32, 51, 59, 65.

Photographs: Photo Edit Inc.: Susan Van Etten: 68; Kayte M. Deioma: 62;
Inmagine: Brand X: 70; Photodisc: 14, 56; Photo Alto: 24; Blend Images: 39;
Index Stock Imagery: Omni Photo Communications Inc.: 72; Getty Images:
Photographers Choice: 72; Asia Images: 25; Dorling Kindersley: 44 (water);
Alamy: Simon Fraser: 72; Worldwide Picture Library: 74; Russ Bishop: 19; Jupiter
Images: Ablestock.com: 72; Photos.com: 28, 35; Comstock.com: 42; Goodshot: 44;
PhotoObjects.net: 46 (carrots, potatoes); Greg Vaughn.com: 72; Robert Stock:
H. Lefebvre: 72; ImageState: 89; Idaho Stock: Steve Bly: 19; Omni Photo: Anita
Brause: 31; Masterfile: Gary Gerovac: 39; Janet Horton: 44 (soda, apples), 46
(water); Tom Pantanges: 44 (ice cream, spaghetti sauce), 46 (salt); Judi DeSouter
for OUP (spaghetti, cookies): 44; Index Open: 46 (butter), 46 (mushrooms); Sylvia
Kucharska: 63.

I am thankful to Vladimir Gorescu, whose love, support,
and encouragement gave me the courage to write this
book. His patience throughout countless evenings and
weekends dedicated to craft this work is remarkable.

I extend my gratitude to my editor, Ashli Totty, for her
guidance. Her flexibility and understanding were critical
in the completion of this work.

Finally, I am deeply grateful to my mother and father,
without whom this manuscript would not have come
into existence. This book is dedicated to them.

Renata Russo

It's been a privilege to work with Step Forward's gifted
team of editors, designers, and authors. Special thanks
to Renata Russo— for all her care and hard work,
to Ashli Totty—for her expertise and good humor,
to Meg Brooks—for her point of view, and to Ingrid
Wisniewska—for the book without which this book
would not be.

For those who love the phrase "Open your workbook."

Jayme Adelson-Goldstein

CONTENTS

Learning to Learn

Vocabulary

A **Match the sentences with the pictures.**

_____ David likes to look up words in the dictionary.

_____ Kalila likes to copy new words in her notebook.

_____ Dan likes to brainstorm words.

__1__ Mei likes to use a computer.

_____ Terrell likes to listen to CDs.

B **Complete the sentences. Use the words in the box.**

~~CD player~~ chart group flashcards the Internet pair

1. Niki listens to English on her _____CD player_____.

2. Two students are working together. That's a _____.

3. Beth often uses the computer and works on _____.

4. There are three students in that _____.

5. Alex likes to use _____ with a partner.

6. Lucas and Moy are making a _____ to brainstorm new words.

A **Complete the paragraph. Use the words in the box.**

use the computer	listen to	a good listener
a partner	on the Internet	copy new words

I like my English class a lot. Every day is different and fun. On Mondays and

Wednesdays, we go to the lab to ____use the computer____. I like to read about

1

new things _____. On Tuesdays, I practice with

2

_____. My partner's name is Lisa. I learn from her, too. On

3

Thursdays, we _____ CDs in class. It helps me understand

4

the new words. I also like to _____ in my notebook. I am

5

_____ in class. I like to listen to my classmates and my teacher.

6

B **How do you practice English? Take the quiz. Check (✔) *yes* or *no*.**

How Do You Practice English?

1 **Do you like to practice with a partner?**
  ☐ yes   ☐ no

2 **Do you read stories in English?**
  ☐ yes   ☐ no

3 **Do you listen to CDs?**
  ☐ yes   ☐ no

4 **Do you listen to TV and radio programs in English?**
  ☐ yes   ☐ no

5 **Do you write letters in English?**
  ☐ yes   ☐ no

6 **Do you look up words in the dictionary?**
  ☐ yes   ☐ no

7 **Do you make charts?**
  ☐ yes   ☐ no

8 **Do you talk with friends and classmates in English?**
  ☐ yes   ☐ no

LOOK AT YOUR ANSWERS: Did you answer . . .
yes to 1, 3, 4, and 8? You like to listen and speak.
yes to 2, 5, 6, and 7? You like to read and write.
yes to more than 6 questions? You practice in many different ways. That's great!
no to more than 6 questions? Try to practice English in more ways. It's fun!

A Complete the sentences. Use the verbs in parentheses.

1. Carlos _____ needs to study _____ grammar. (need, study)

2. Linda _____ at home. (want, work)

3. Maria and Monica _____ at night. (like, study)

4. They _____ the computer. (need, use)

5. I _____ alone. (want, work)

B Look at the pictures. Answer the questions. Write 2 sentences.

1. Does Rosa like to study in the evening?

   Rosa doesn't like to study in the
   evening.
   She likes to study in the morning.

3. Does Yoshi like to study alone?

   _____

   _____

   _____

2. Do they need to study the simple past?

   _____

   _____

   _____

4. Does Fernando want a math book?

   _____

   _____

   _____

C Unscramble the questions.

1. like to study / What / you / do

   <u>What do you like to study?</u>

2. Brenda / How does / like to learn

   _____

3. they / do / When / need to study

   _____

4. Where /she / want to meet / does

   _____

D Match the questions with the answers.

<u>d</u>   1. What does she like to study?   a. He wants to meet at the library.

____   2. Where does he want to meet?   b. He wants to study with a partner.

____   3. When do you need to study?   c. I need to study tonight.

____   4. How does David want to study?   d. She likes to study grammar.

E 🚀 **Grammar Boost**   **Complete the sentences. Circle a or b.**

1. I _____ in class yesterday.

   ⓐ was

   b. am

2. Lisa and Adam _____ at home now.

   a. were

   b. are

3. He _____ sick last week.

   a. was

   b. is

4. We _____ in Europe last month.

   a. were

   b. are

5. Helen _____ in school now.

   a. was

   b. is

> **Need help?**
>
> **Time expressions**
> Present
>   today
>   now
>
> Past
>   yesterday
>   last week
>   last month
>   last year

A Complete the conversation. Use the words in the box.

> Hi, everyone
> It's nice to meet
> your name
> How do you

Carlos: _Hi, everyone_ . I want to introduce my friend, Nadim Ali.
       1

Teresa: What's _____ again?
                              2

Nadim: Nadim Ali.

Teresa: _____ spell your first name?
                      3

Nadim: N-A-D-I-M.

Teresa: _____ you, Nadim.
                      4

Nadim: Nice to meet you, too.

B Complete the conversation.

Vashon: Hi, I'm Vashon Evans.

Wendy: I'm sorry. _What's your name_ again?
                            1

Vashon: Vashon.

Wendy: How _____ your first name?
                      2

Vashon: V-A-S-H-O-N. What's your name?

Wendy: My name is Wendy Chow.

Vashon: How _____ your last name?
                       3

Wendy: C-H-O-W.

Vashon: Oh. Nice to meet you.

Wendy: Nice _____, too.
                       4

C 🖩 **Real-life math** Answer the question.

There are 35 students in Ms. Smith's English class. Their first languages are Spanish, Japanese, Portuguese, and Arabic. Fifteen students speak Spanish. Ten students speak Japanese. Only two students speak Portuguese.

How many students speak Arabic? _____

LESSON 5   Real-life reading

A   Read the article.

Personal Goals

Goals are important in school and work. It's important to make a plan for your goals. A plan can have many steps. Here are two examples of personal goals:

- Go on a vacation.
  Step 1. Save money for the vacation every month.
  Step 2. Open a bank account.
- Be more social.
  Step 1. Meet new people.
  Step 2. Make a new friend.

Write down your goals. Make plans for your goals. Review your goals every week.

B   Read the goals in the chart. Then complete the chart with two steps for each goal. Use the ideas below.

- Bring my lunch to work 3 days a week.
- Go out for coffee with my classmates.
- Learn to use a computer.
- Have a party for my neighbors.
- Play with my kids every evening.
- Take a vacation with my family.
- Put $5 in the bank every week.
- Take a class in house repairs.

Goal: Be a good parent.	Goal: Save $25 every month.
1. Take a vacation with my family.	1.
2.	2.
Goal: Learn a new skill.	Goal: Make new friends.
1.	1.
2.	2.

C   What about you? Write one of your personal goals. Then write two steps for the goal.

My Goal: _____

Step 1: _____

Step 2: _____

A **Find the words in the puzzle. Circle them.**

| flashcards | ~~practice~~ | chart | listener | plan |
| education | steps | goal | recipe | brainstorm |

E	V	G	O	A	L	U	L	I	K	B	T	V
G	Y	N	U	L	I	S	T	E	N	E	R	F
U	M	I	L	O	P	T	E	W	A	Z	X	L
H	G	E	N	T	P	O	C	U	C	E	M	A
S	I	D	U	H	K	N	F	R	I	D	G	S
T	N	U	H	I	F	C	H	A	R	T	Z	H
E	Z	C	W	X	C	A	B	N	E	A	K	C
P	L	A	N	X	L	R	G	R	C	D	E	A
S	Y	T	B	X	J	S	D	E	I	F	T	R
H	B	I	J	N	T	E	U	U	P	N	V	D
E	R	O	N	X	Y	P	T	E	E	O	I	S
B	S	N	B	R	A	I	N	S	T	O	R	M
P	R	A	C	T	I	C	E	W	E	X	R	T

B **Complete the sentences. Use the words in the puzzle.**

1. I like to __practice__ vocabulary words with _____.

2. They're making a _____ with new words.

3. Do you like to _____ new words with your classmates?

4. I want to learn a new language. That's my _____.

5. There are three _____ in my _____ for this goal.

6. I'm a good _____, but speaking is difficult for me.

7. The chef wants to try a new _____ for chocolate cookies.

8. It's important to get a good _____.

Getting Together

A **Complete the sentences. Circle *a* or *b*.**

1. I'm ____. There's nothing to do here.

   a. cheerful

   b. bored

2. Steve is very tired. He's ____.

   a. sleepy

   b. surprised

3. Mei gives Alison some flowers for her birthday. Alison is ____.

   a. upset

   b. surprised

4. The students are all late for class today. The teacher is ____.

   a. bored

   b. upset

5. Fernando can't understand the new words. He's ____.

   a. happy

   b. frustrated

B **Complete the sentences. Use the words in the box.**

thunderstorm	snowstorm	freezing	~~foggy~~	icy	hot

1.  I can't see the house across the street. It's very ___foggy___.

2.  Be careful! Don't fall. The streets are _____ today.

3.  Look at the lightning! This is a bad _____.

4.  It's cold and cloudy today. We're going to have a _____.

5.  It's often humid in the summer. It's _____, too.

6.  Brr! It's _____ outside today. I'm wearing my winter coat.

LESSON 2 Life stories

A Complete the paragraph. Use the words in the box.

his vacation	some friends	cool and sunny
~~favorite season~~	beautiful fall days	to go for walks

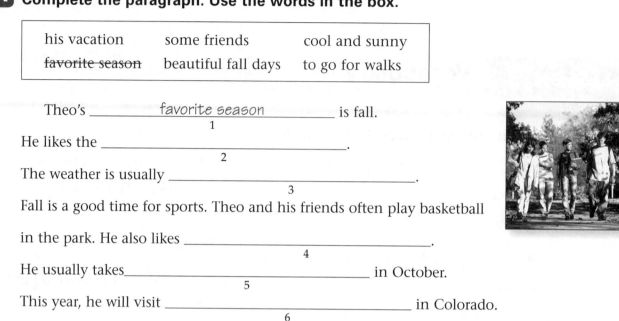

Theo's _____favorite season_____ is fall.
                              1
He likes the _____.
                              2
The weather is usually _____.
                              3
Fall is a good time for sports. Theo and his friends often play basketball

in the park. He also likes _____.
                              4
He usually takes_____ in October.
                              5
This year, he will visit _____ in Colorado.
                              6

B Read the calendar. Answer the questions. Use complete sentences.

October

Sun.	Mon.	Tues.	Wed.	Thurs.	Fri.	Sat.
1 art festival	2	3	4	5	6	7 county fair
8	9 Theo's vacation begins	10	11	12	13	14 basketball game

1. When is the art festival?

   It's on Sunday, October 1st.

   _____

2. When is the basketball game?

   _____

   _____

3. When is the first day of Theo's vacation?

   _____

   _____

4. When is the county fair?

   _____

   _____

A **Complete the sentences. Use *will* or *won't* and the verbs in parentheses.**

1. The concert _____will start_____ at 9:00 p.m. (start)

2. They _____ to the movies with me. (not / go)

3. We _____ them at the party in July. (see)

4. She _____ on vacation in January. (be)

5. He _____ his family in California in November. (visit)

6. The concert _____ before 10 p.m. (not / end)

B **Read Walter's calendar. These sentences are false. Write the correct information.**

1. Walter will start school in February.

   _Walter won't start school in February._____

   _He'll start school in March._____

2. Walter will go to his brother's graduation in March.

   _____

   _____

3. Walter will visit his parents in January.

   _____

   _____

4. Walter will go on vacation in April.

   _____

   _____

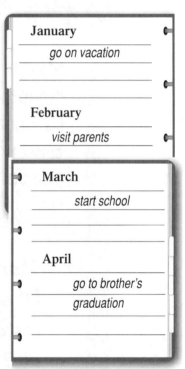

January
go on vacation

February
visit parents

March
start school

April
go to brother's
graduation

C **Match the questions with the answers.**

_e_ 1. When will they be back?   a. I'll be at work.

____ 2. When will Julia start school?   b. He'll go for a walk tomorrow.

____ 3. When will we be on vacation?   c. She'll start school in September.

____ 4. When will he go for a walk?   d. We'll be on vacation in July.

____ 5. Where will you be at this   e. They'll be back in May.
time tomorrow?

D **Answer the questions. Circle *a* or *b*.**

1. When will she start school?
   a. She'll start school in the fall.
   b. Yes, she will.

2. Will they go to the concert?
   a. It'll start at 5:00 p.m.
   b. Yes, they will.

3. When will Peter go on vacation?
   a. He'll go in December.
   b. No, he won't.

4. Where will you be at this time next week?
   a. I am at work.
   b. I'll be at work.

5. Where will they be five years from now?
   a. They're in New York.
   b. They'll be in New York.

E **Grammar Boost** **Read the notes. Write sentences with *will* or *won't*.**

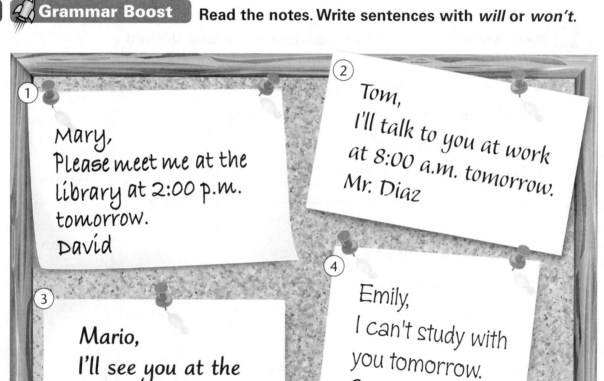

1. Mary, Please meet me at the library at 2:00 p.m. tomorrow. David

2. Tom, I'll talk to you at work at 8:00 a.m. tomorrow. Mr. Diaz

3. Mario, I'll see you at the restaurant tomorrow at 7:00 p.m. Phil

4. Emily, I can't study with you tomorrow. Sorry! Don

1. _Mary will meet David at the library tomorrow at 2:00 p.m._

2. _____

3. _____

4. _____

A Look at the map. Complete the conversation. Use the words in the box.

Go up	the bridge	~~How can I get~~	Go straight
that's it	turn right	next to	

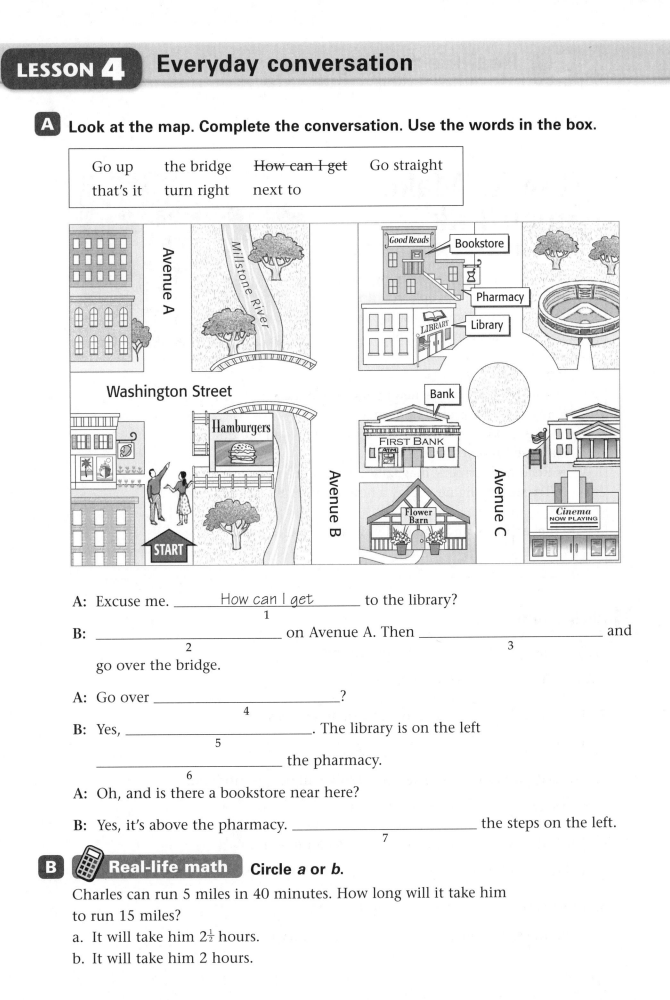

A: Excuse me. _____How can I get_____ to the library?
                              1

B: _____ on Avenue A. Then _____ and
                  2   3
go over the bridge.

A: Go over _____?
                          4

B: Yes, _____. The library is on the left
                    5
_____ the pharmacy.
              6

A: Oh, and is there a bookstore near here?

B: Yes, it's above the pharmacy. _____ the steps on the left.
                                                      7

B **Real-life math** Circle **a** or **b**.

Charles can run 5 miles in 40 minutes. How long will it take him
to run 15 miles?

a. It will take him $2\frac{1}{2}$ hours.

b. It will take him 2 hours.

A Read the article.

How To Make
Small Talk

Do you feel nervous with strangers? Is it difficult to talk to people you don't know? Here are some ideas that will make small talk easier for you.

1. Practice.
- Talk with everyone: neighbors, classmates, restaurant servers, children, everyone!
- Be a good listener. You don't have to talk all the time!

2. Have good topics for small talk.
- Read newspapers, magazines, books, signs, everything.
- Try something new! Play a new sport. Eat a different food.

Do these things, and you will have a lot to talk about!

B Circle *a* or *b*.

1. Some people feel _____ with large groups.

   a. difficult   b. nervous

2. The article has _____ ideas to make small talk easy.

   a. one   b. two

3. Talk with other people. Then small talk will be _____ for you.

   a. easier   b. more difficult

4. The article says you can get ideas for small talk from _____.

   a. books and newspapers   b. your homework

5. To have small talk topics, it's important to _____.

   a. do the same things   b. try something new

Complete the sentences. Use the words in the box. Then complete the puzzle.

weather	frustrated	vacation	icy	Thunderstorms
festival	mood	bored	cool	~~over~~

Across

1. Go ____*over*____ the bridge on First Street.

4. This book isn't interesting. I'm _____.

6. Be careful! The sidewalk is _____.

8. Do you want to go to the music _____?

9. Look at the lightning! _____ can be dangerous.

10. Are you in the _____ for conversation?

Down

2. Steve will go to Hawaii on _____ in December.

3. He's very _____. His car won't start.

5. It's _____ in here. I need a sweater.

7. The _____ will be hot and humid tomorrow.

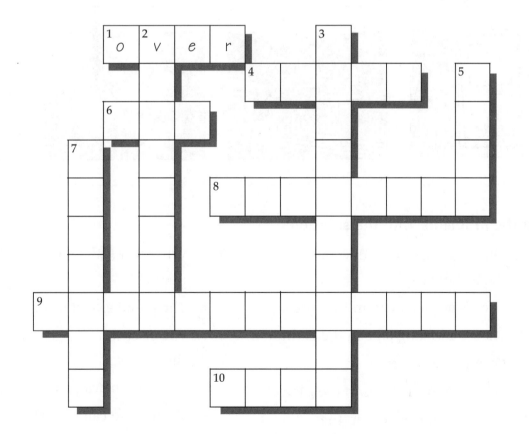

Moving Out

LESSON 1 **Vocabulary**

A Match the words with the pictures. Use the words in the box.

| leaking pipe | no electricity | ~~cracked window~~ |
| mice | dripping faucet | broken door |

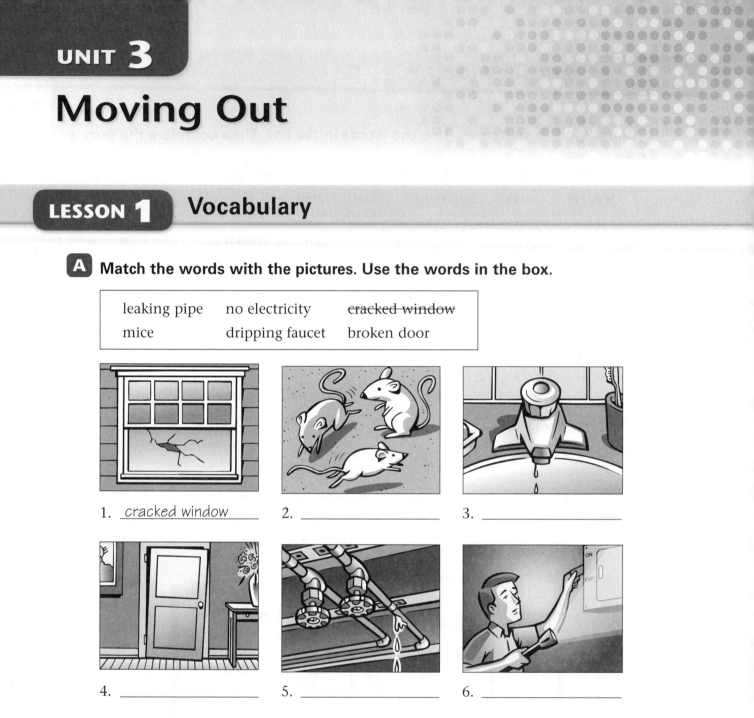

1. _cracked window_   2. _____   3. _____

4. _____   5. _____   6. _____

B Match the problems with the solutions.

_f_ 1. There's a cracked window in the bedroom.

____ 2. There's no electricity in the basement.

____ 3. There's a leaking pipe in the bathroom.

____ 4. I can't find my key.

____ 5. There are cockroaches in the garage.

____ 6. There's a broken door in the living room.

a. What is the locksmith's phone number?

b. The plumber will be here soon.

c. The electrician will check the fuse box.

d. Let's call the carpenter.

e. We need to call the exterminator.

f. The repair person will fix it.

A Complete the paragraph. Use the words in the box.

have two	There was also	small apartment	the big house
for the children	very sunny	~~had a big family~~	five bedrooms

Mr. and Mrs. Smith lived in a big house. They _____had a big family_____

with six children! There were _____ and three bathrooms in the
                                            2

house. _____ a large yard around the house. The children played
                     3

there every afternoon.

Now the Smith's children don't live at home. The Smiths don't need

_____. So, now they live in a _____ in a
              4   5

nice neighborhood. The living room has many windows, and it's _____.
                                                                                              6

They _____ bedrooms. One bedroom is for Mr. and Mrs. Smith. The
              7

other is _____ when they visit. Mr. and Mrs. Smith are happy in their
                     8

new apartment.

B Read the ads. Mark the sentences T (true) or F (false).

Ⓐ **Apartment for rent**

1BR/1BA apt, 1st floor, nr school
$600/mo. $250 sec. dep.
Call mgr at (250) 555-3000

Ⓑ **Apartment for rent**

Lg 2BR/1BA apt, 3rd floor
$700/mo. $300 sec. dep.
Call mgr at (250) 555-6363

__F__ 1. Apartment A has two bedrooms.

_____ 2. The rent for apartment B is $700 a month.

_____ 3. There is a $250 security deposit for apartment A.

_____ 4. Apartment B is a small apartment.

_____ 5. There is no security deposit for apartment B.

_____ 6. Apartment A is on the 3rd floor.

A Complete the chart.

Adjective	Comparative
1. safe	safer
2. dangerous	more dangerous
3. small	
4. pretty	
5. convenient	
6. quiet	
7. expensive	
8. noisy	
9. large	
10. bad	

B Look at the pictures. Write sentences about the two apartments.
Use the comparative form of the adjectives in parentheses.

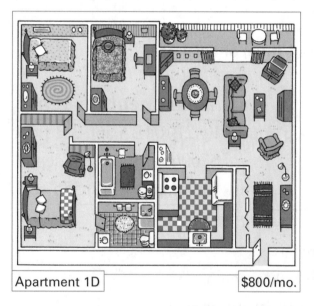

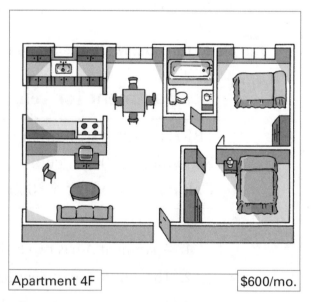

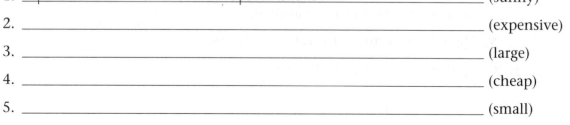

Apartment 1D — $800/mo.   Apartment 4F — $600/mo.

1. __Apartment 4F is sunnier than apartment 1D._____ (sunny)

2. _____ (expensive)

3. _____ (large)

4. _____ (cheap)

5. _____ (small)

C **Complete the questions. Then write your opinion.**

1. Which is <u>colder, the house or the cabin</u> ?
   (cold)
   <u>I think the cabin is colder than the house</u> .

2. Which is _____ ?
   (sunny)

   _____ .

3. Which is _____ ?
   (big)

   _____ .

log cabin

4. Which is _____ ?
   (pretty)

   _____ .

5. Which is _____ ?
   (comfortable)

   _____ .

adobe house

6. Which is _____ ?
   (expensive)

   _____ .

D 🚀 **Grammar Boost** **Write one sentence using the two sentences.**
Use _and_ or _but_.

1. The house is convenient. It isn't sunny.
   <u>The house is convenient, but it isn't sunny.</u>

2. Her house is near the school. It's near the bus stop.
   <u>Her house is near the school, and it's near</u>
   <u>the bus stop.</u>

3. The apartment has a big living room. The kitchen is very small.

   _____

   _____

4. The apartment is large. It is near a shopping center.

   _____

   _____

> **Need help?**
>
> **And/But**
> To make one sentence from two sentences with similar ideas, use _and_.
>
> To make one sentence from two sentences with different ideas, use _but_.

A **Read the ad. Complete the conversation.**

Brian: Hey, Karen. Here's an apartment for rent.

Karen: Oh, really? How much is it?

Brian: It's _$700 a month_ .
                              1

Karen: That's a little expensive. How many bedrooms does the apartment have?

Brian: It has _____.
                              2
           The apartment is on the _____ floor.
                                                    3

Karen: Is there a _____?
                              4

Brian: Yes, the security deposit is _____.
                                                    5

Karen: That sounds great! Let's see it.

Apartment for rent

Lg 2BR/2BA apt 1st floor nr sch

$700/mo. $350 sec. dep., utils. incl.

Call mgr at (205) 555-2221

B **Match the questions with the answers.**

_c_ 1. How many bedrooms does the house have?

___ 2. Is there a security deposit?

___ 3. How much is the rent?

___ 4. Are utilities included?

___ 5. When is the apartment available?

___ 6. Is there parking?

a. It's available next month.

b. It's $850 a month.

c. It has three bedrooms.

d. Yes, there are two spaces.

e. Yes, it's $500.

f. No, they're not.

C **Real-life math** **Circle a or b.**

Steve's rent is $500 a month. The security deposit is $200. How much will Steve spend on rent in one year including the deposit?

a. $6,000

b. $6,200

A **Answer the questions about yourself.**

1. Do you live in a small town or a big city?
2. Which is better, a small town or a big city?

B **Read the magazine article.**

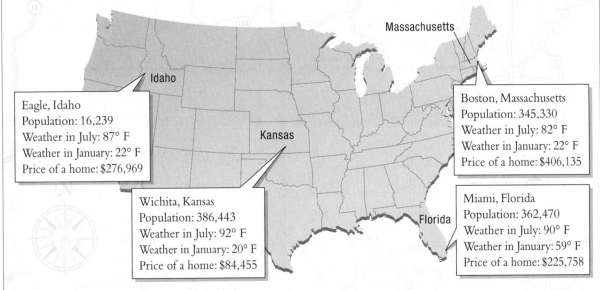

Where do YOU want to live?

Where do you want to live? In a big city? In a small town? Which is better? Here at *Population Magazine*, we give you the information you need. Get the facts, and get ready to move!

Massachusetts

Idaho

Eagle, Idaho
Population: 16,239
Weather in July: 87° F
Weather in January: 22° F
Price of a home: $276,969

Kansas

Boston, Massachusetts
Population: 345,330
Weather in July: 82° F
Weather in January: 22° F
Price of a home: $406,135

Wichita, Kansas
Population: 386,443
Weather in July: 92° F
Weather in January: 20° F
Price of a home: $84,455

Florida

Miami, Florida
Population: 362,470
Weather in July: 90° F
Weather in January: 59° F
Price of a home: $225,758

C **Answer the questions. Use complete sentences.**

1. Which city is hotter, Miami or Wichita?

   Wichita is hotter than Miami.

2. Which city has a larger population, Boston or Miami?

   _____

3. Which city has a smaller population, Eagle or Wichita?

   _____

4. Which city has more expensive houses, Boston or Wichita?

   _____

5. Which city has cheaper houses, Eagle or Miami?

   _____

Unscramble the words.

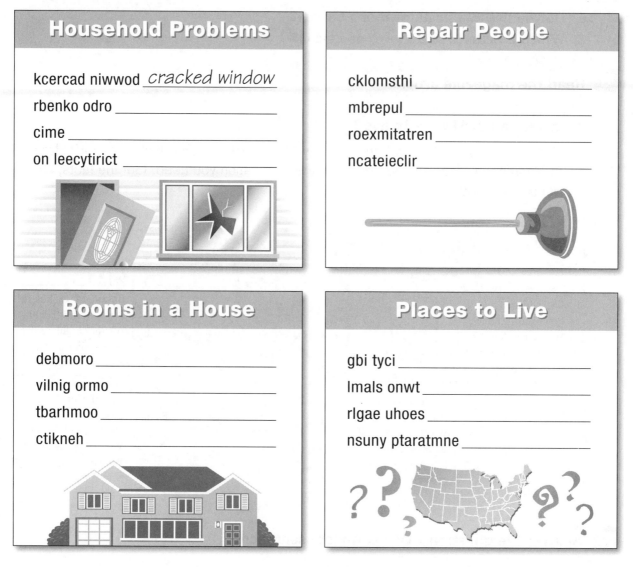

Household Problems

kcercad niwwod _cracked window_

rbenko odro _____

cime _____

on leecytirict _____

Repair People

cklomsthi _____

mbrepul _____

roexmitatren _____

ncateieclir _____

Rooms in a House

debmoro _____

vilnig ormo _____

tbarhmoo _____

ctikneh _____

Places to Live

gbi tyci _____

lmals onwt _____

rlgae uhoes _____

nsuny ptaratmne _____

Looking for Work

Vocabulary

A Look at the job application. Write the names of the sections. Use the words in the box.

Employment history	Job skills	References	Education	~~Personal information~~

APPLICATION FOR EMPLOYMENT

1. Personal Information

Name: (last, first, middle initial)
Hernandez, Carla M

Address: (street, city, state)
301 Melo Road
San Jose, CA

Telephone: (901) 555-0102

3. _____

Jobs: (position, employer, dates)
Assistant manager, Lee's Supermarket, 2005-present
Cashier, Lee's Supermarket, 2003-2005

2. _____

Name of institution: (dates)
WRC Community College: 2002-2004

4. _____

Languages:
English, Spanish, Italian
Can you use a computer? (yes) no

5. _____
(name, relation, contact)
Paul Lee, boss, (901) 555-3967
Gloria Vega, teacher, (901) 555-2843

B Who says these things? Match the sentences with the jobs.

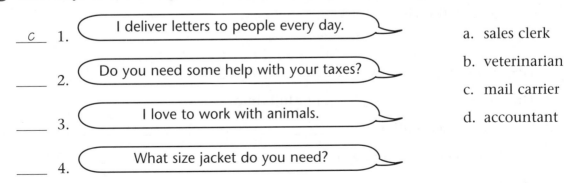

_c_ 1. I deliver letters to people every day.

____ 2. Do you need some help with your taxes?

____ 3. I love to work with animals.

____ 4. What size jacket do you need?

a. sales clerk

b. veterinarian

c. mail carrier

d. accountant

A **Complete the paragraph. Use the words in the box.**

be nervous	job interviews	~~job skills~~	a suit and tie
the interviewer	make eye contact	on time	clean and neat

Rosa teaches a _____job skills_____ class.
1

Here are some of the tips she gives her students

about _____.
2

- Be _____ for the interview.
3
Don't be late!

- Your clothes should be _____.
4

- Men should wear _____. Women should wear a skirt.
5

- Smile and say hello to _____.
6

- You should _____ when you shake hands. Don't
7
look at the floor.

- Finally, don't _____!
8

Follow these simple rules that Rosa gives her students, and you'll get the job!

B **Read the job ad. Complete the sentences. Use complete words, not abbreviations.**

> **Accountant**
>
> P/T, five yrs. accounting exp. req.
> Fax employment history and refs. to
> 1-800-555-4392. No phone calls please.
> Start immed. Billy Craig Company

1. The Billy Craig Company needs an _____accountant_____.

2. The job is _____, not full-time.

3. Five years of accounting _____ is _____ for this job.

4. You need to fax your employment history and _____ to 1-800-555-4392.

5. The job starts _____.

A Complete the sentences. Use the simple past of the verbs in parentheses.

1. Last night, our family _____ate_____ dinner together. (eat)

2. At the table, we _____ about our day. (talk)

3. Our son _____ a good grade on his English test yesterday. (get)

4. My husband _____ to a Spanish class after work. (go)

5. Our daughter _____ for a job at the supermarket today. (apply)

6. After dinner, I _____ a letter to my friends in Miami. (write)

B Complete the sentences. Then write negative sentences. Use the simple past and words in parentheses.

1. We _____took_____ Italian classes in January and February. (take)

   _We didn't take Spanish classes._____ (Spanish)

2. Alicia _____ a job interview at the post office yesterday. (have)

   _____ (bank)

3. Steve _____ at the National Bank for six months. (work)

   _____ (Roy's Supermarket)

4. Melissa _____ a job at the supermarket. (get)

   _____ (post office)

5. Jon _____ a job application for a job at the gas station. (fill out)

   _____ (library)

6. I _____ two books in July. (read)

   _____ (the newspaper)

C Read the job applications. Unscramble the *Yes/No* questions. Then write the answers. Use the simple past.

JOB APPLICATION
Personal Information
Name:
Keisha Washington
Employment history:
Accountant: State Bank (from 1998 to 2004)

JOB APPLICATION
Personal Information
Name:
Gao Wang
Education:
B.A. University of California (2001)
Employment history:
Teacher: Lewis Elementary School (from 2001-2003)

1. at / Keisha / work / Did / bank / a

   A: _Did Keisha work at a bank_____?

   B: _Yes, she did_____.

2. ten / work / years / Keisha / State Bank / for / at / Did

   A: _____?

   B: _____.

3. Gao / the University of Pennsylvania / Did / graduate from

   A: _____?

   B: _____.

4. years / Gao / three / work at / Did / Lewis Elementary School / for

   A: _____?

   B: _____.

D 🚀 **Grammar Boost** Write sentences. Use the words from each column.

Column 1	Column 2	Column 3
~~She's~~	have experience	last year
He was	~~good~~	~~at languages~~
They	got their GEDs	at the store on the corner
We	a cashier	using computers

_She's good at languages._____

_____

_____

_____

LESSON 4 Everyday conversation

A Read John's job application.

Application for Employment	
Name: John Smith	
Experience: 2 years as an office manager at BZD, Inc.	**Education:** Bachelor's degree in Computer Science
Special skills: computers, good at working with people	**Reference:** Carla Santiago, President of BZD, Inc.

B Look at the application in A. Complete the conversation.

Interviewer: Tell me about your education.

John: I have a _bachelor's_ degree in _____.
                                  1   2

Interviewer: How much experience do you have?

John: I worked for _____ years as an _____.
                                  3   4

Interviewer: Do you have any special skills?

John: I'm good at _____ and working _____.
                                  5   6

Interviewer: Do you have any references?

John: Yes, I do. _____ will give me a reference. She's the
                              7

president of BZD, Inc.

C **Real-life math** Answer the questions. Use the information in the chart.

Name	Job/Employer	Dates
Rita	chef / Hotel Royale	January 1, 1987–December 31, 1991
George	computer programmer / BZD, Inc.	March 1, 1999–September, 31 2003

1. How long did Rita work as a chef at the Hotel Royale?

   She worked as a chef at the Hotel Royale for five years.

2. How long did George work as a computer programmer at BZD, Inc.?

   _____

Unit 4 Lesson 4 **27**

A Read about John's career plans.

Planning for Success

John Fernandez

Many high school graduates need advice about how to get a good job. Career counselors give job advice. They give suggestions on how to set and reach career goals.

John Fernandez graduated from high school in June. He got a job as an office assistant in July. He wants to be a computer programmer one day. A career counselor gave John some advice. He told him to make a plan. Here is John's plan:

1. He's going to take classes at a community college in the evenings.
2. He's going to take computer classes on Saturdays.
3. He'll get a bachelor's degree in Computer Science.

John plans to reach his career goals. He knows he can do it!

B Look at A. Circle *a* or *b*.

1. John graduated from ____.
   a. college
   (b.) high school

2. He got a job as ____.
   a. an office assistant
   b. a career counselor

3. He plans to take classes at a community college ____.
   a. in the morning
   b. in the evening

4. John's going to take ____ on Saturdays.
   a. computer classes
   b. science classes

5. John plans to get ____ in Computer Science.
   a. an associate's degree
   b. a bachelor's degree

Kate wants to apply for a new job. She has education and work experience. But Kate is not very organized! Help Kate complete this job application. Use her notes to help.

State – bachelor's degree 2000–2002

✻Assistant Manager, Flynn's Restaurant, 2002–2004

- I can use computers.
- Simm's Restaurant Service 2004–present
- Jennifer's phone number: (303) 555-2134

From: kate@internet.us
To: ewilson52@net.us
Subject: New Apartment!

Hi Mom,
My new apartment is great! Here's my new address and phone number: 2121 Post Street, Denver, Colorado 80202, (303) 555-7750. I'll see you soon!
Love,
Kate

- Languages: English, Spanish

✻City Community College, 1998–2000 associate's degree Denver

JOB APPLICATION

Personal Infomation

NAME (LAST/FIRST)			
Wilson, Kate			
ADDRESS (NUMBER/STREET)	(CITY)	(STATE)	
		Colorado	
TELEPHONE (DAY)	(EVENING)		
(303) 555-6520			
EMAIL			
kate@internet.us			

Employment History (Start with most recent job)

EMPLOYER 1 (NAME)	(POSITION)	(DATES)	(CITY/STATE)
	Manager		Denver, Colorado
EMPLOYER 2 (NAME)	(POSITION)	(DATES)	(CITY/STATE)
		2002–2004	Denver, Colorado

Education (Start with most recent)

SCHOOL 1 (NAME)	(DEGREE)	(DATES)	(CITY/STATE)
State University			Denver, Colorado
SCHOOL 2 (NAME)	(DEGREE)	(DATES)	(CITY/STATE)
	associate's degree		

Job Skills

COMPUTER SKILLS	LANGUAGES
☐ YES ☐ NO	

Reference

NAME	RELATION/CONTACT	PHONE #
Jennifer Long	Employer	

On the Job

LESSON 1 **Vocabulary**

A **Complete the chart. Use the words in the box.**

hourly rate	~~gross pay~~	net pay
federal tax	Social Security	pay period

Kinds of pay	Deductions	Earnings
gross pay		

B **Look at the picture. Check (✓) what you see.**

✓ printer

____ computer

____ photocopier

____ file cabinet

____ vending machine

____ scanner

____ time clock

____ fax machine

C **Look at the picture in B. Complete the questions.**

1. A: Where is the _____*printer*_____?

   B: It's on the desk.

2. A: Where is the _____?

   B: It's between the printer and the fax machine.

3. A: Where is the _____?

   B: It's to the right of the computer.

4. A: Where is the _____?

   B: It's next to the file cabinet.

A **Complete the paragraphs. Use the words in the box.**

| the deductions | ~~rules~~ | on time | a uniform |
| time clock | net pay | pay period | needs to |

Samir works as a cashier at a supermarket. In his first week,

he learned some _____rules_____. He has to be
                        1

_____, and he has to wear _____.
         2   3

Samir also _____ smile at the customers.
                        4

Finally, every morning Samir needs to put his time card in the

_____.
         5

The _____ is seven days. Samir always looks
                        6

carefully at _____ and his _____.
                        7   8

Samir works a lot. He needs money to go to college next year.

B **Where is this behavior appropriate? Check (✓) *Work, School,* or *Both* in the chart.**

Behavior	Work	School	Both
1. Wear a hard hat	✓		
2. Don't be late			
3. Wear appropriate clothing			
4. Ask the teacher for help			
5. Be nice to customers			
6. No drinks near computers			

A Unscramble the sentences. Then write the negative.

1. be angry / might / He / with me

   <u>He might be angry with me.</u>

   <u>He might not be angry with me.</u>

2. might / a raise / get / She

   _____

   _____

3. for work / might / I / be late

   _____

   _____

4. make / They / a mistake / might

   _____

   _____

B Look at the pictures. Complete the sentences. Use *might* or *might not* and the verbs in parentheses.

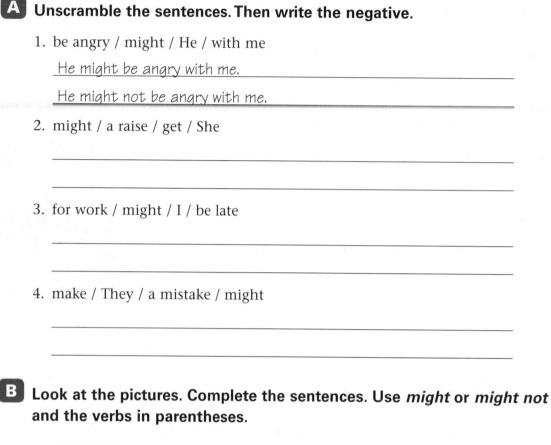

1. Marco _____<u>might ask</u>_____ his coworker for help. (ask)

2. Steve _____ home early today. (go)

3. Marco _____ fired. (get)

4. Steve _____ a raise. (get)

5. Marco _____ his work on time. (finish)

6. Steve _____ his coworker. (help)

C **Linda has a job interview tomorrow. Complete the charts. Use *should* or *shouldn't* and the words in the box.**

be late	~~make eye contact~~	shake hands
be nervous	~~make a mistake~~	ask questions

Things Linda should do

She should make eye contact.

Things Linda shouldn't do

She shouldn't make a mistake.

D 🚀 **Grammar Boost** **Complete the paragraphs. Use the words in the boxes. Use each word or words once.**

have to	might	~~shouldn't~~

1. Tom isn't wearing his hard hat. He ___shouldn't___ go into the delivery area.
                                 ₁

   All workers in the delivery area _____ wear hard hats. What's Tom
                                              ₂

   going to do? He _____ go home for his hat.
                          ₃

might	might not	shouldn't

2. Joe's driving to work, and it's snowing. Joe _____ drive too fast.
                                               ₄

   He _____ have an accident. He _____ get to work on
          ₅   ₆

   time, but his boss will understand.

A Complete the conversation. Use the words in the box.

scan these	make copies	right away
that letter	~~write an email~~	use the forklift

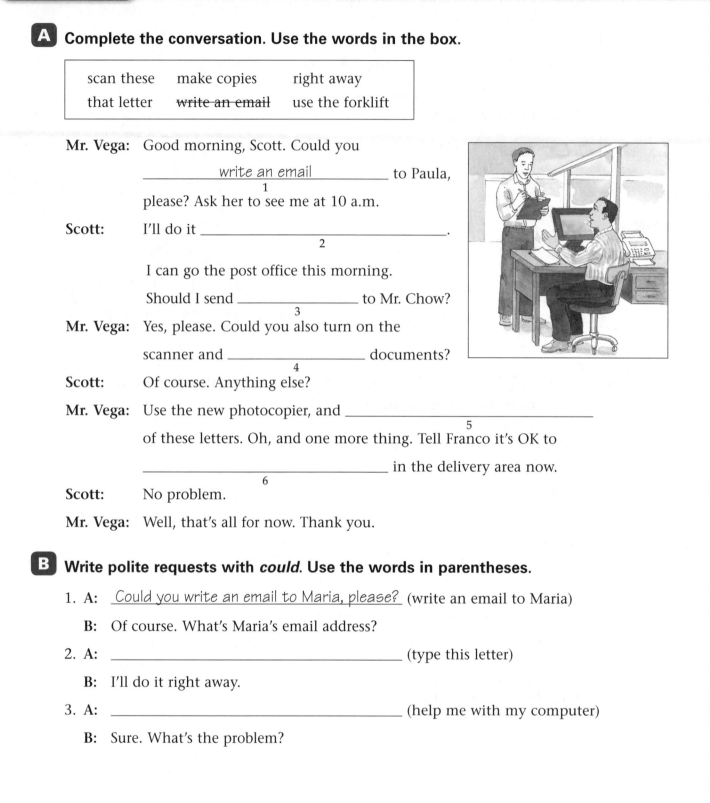

Mr. Vega: Good morning, Scott. Could you

_____ write an email _____ to Paula,

1

please? Ask her to see me at 10 a.m.

Scott: I'll do it _____.

2

I can go the post office this morning.

Should I send _____ to Mr. Chow?

3

Mr. Vega: Yes, please. Could you also turn on the

scanner and _____ documents?

4

Scott: Of course. Anything else?

Mr. Vega: Use the new photocopier, and _____

5

of these letters. Oh, and one more thing. Tell Franco it's OK to

_____ in the delivery area now.

6

Scott: No problem.

Mr. Vega: Well, that's all for now. Thank you.

B Write polite requests with *could*. Use the words in parentheses.

1. **A:** _Could you write an email to Maria, please?_ (write an email to Maria)

   B: Of course. What's Maria's email address?

2. **A:** _____ (type this letter)

   B: I'll do it right away.

3. **A:** _____ (help me with my computer)

   B: Sure. What's the problem?

A Read the article.

GET A GOOD JOB EVALUATION

Here are some things you can do to get a good job evaluation.

- *Show a positive attitude.* A negative attitude doesn't help anyone.
- *Don't complain about little things.* Maybe you can fix the problem. Talk to a coworker and find a solution.
- *Be friendly to customers and coworkers.* Smile at customers. Don't be angry with coworkers.
- *Show that you want to learn new things.* For example, ask questions about the new computer. Try to use the scanner.
- *Cooperate with coworkers.* Show that you want to work with coworkers.
- *Show that you are a hard worker.* Finish your work. Then help others.
- *Follow important safety and health rules.* Be sure you understand all the company rules.
- *Listen carefully to instructions.* Ask for help when you don't understand.
- *Be on time for work.* Don't be late. If you are sick, call your manager.

B Priya read the article above and then did everything right at work. Later she got a very good evaluation. Complete Priya's job evaluation.

Job Evaluation

Employee name: _Priya Singh_

1. __√__ Shows a positive attitude
   ____ Shows a negative attitude

2. ____ Complains often about little things
   ____ Doesn't complain about little things

3. ____ Wants to learn new things
   ____ Doesn't want to learn new things

4. ____ Is a hard worker
   ____ Is not a hard worker

5. ____ Follows important rules
   ____ Doesn't follow important rules

6. ____ Is late for work
   ____ Is on time for work

A Look at the pictures. What is in Fernando's office? What is in Ping's office? What is in both offices? Write F (Fernando's office), P (Ping's office), or B (both).

Fernando's office

Ping's office

___B___ computer   _____ scanner   _____ time clock

_____ fax machine   _____ photocopier   _____ safety glasses

_____ printer   _____ window   _____ file cabinet

B Complete sentences about the pictures in A. Use the words in A.

Fernando's office

1. The _____ time clock _____ is over the file cabinet.

2. The _____ is to the left of the computer.

3. The _____ is next to the printer.

Ping's office

4. The _____ are to the left of the time clock.

5. The _____ is on the file cabinet.

6. The _____ is to the right of the file cabinet.

UNIT 6

Pick Up the Phone

LESSON 1 Vocabulary

A Look at the phone bill. Answer the questions.

1. What were Monica's previous charges?

   <u>$48.16</u>

2. How much does she pay for local service?

   _____

3. What are the two kinds of long distance calls?

   _____

   _____

4. What is the total due on her bill?

   _____

CTCOMMUNICATIONS))	
Monica Ruiz	
(713) 555-1171	Page No. 1 of 1
Previous charges	$48.16
Payment received–Thanks!	$48.16
CURRENT CHARGES	
Local service	$24.00
Long distance calls	
Domestic	$12.50
International	$16.00
Total Due	**$52.50**

B Look at the pictures. Complete the sentences. Use the words in the box.

pay phone	a message	~~cordless phone~~	answering machine
a taxi	cell phone	emergency services	~~directory assistance~~

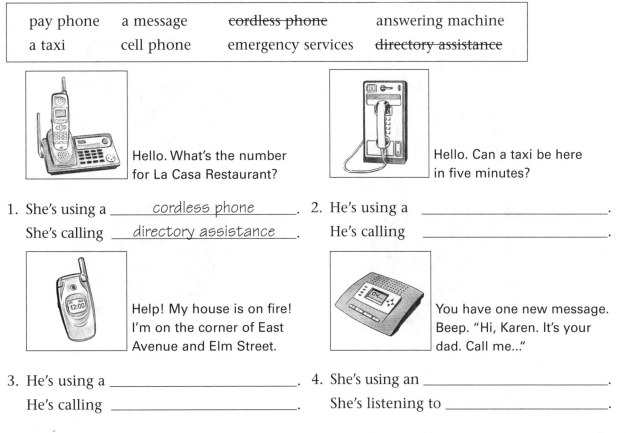

Hello. What's the number for La Casa Restaurant?

Hello. Can a taxi be here in five minutes?

Help! My house is on fire! I'm on the corner of East Avenue and Elm Street.

You have one new message. Beep. "Hi, Karen. It's your dad. Call me…"

1. She's using a <u>cordless phone</u>.
   She's calling <u>directory assistance</u>.

2. He's using a _____.
   He's calling _____.

3. He's using a _____.
   He's calling _____.

4. She's using an _____.
   She's listening to _____.

A Complete the paragraphs about Tara. Use the words in the box.

to get fired	a bad cold	~~to call in sick~~
had to stay	is angry	sick child

Tara works at a bank, and she has three children. She doesn't like _to call in sick_ ,

1

but sometimes she needs to. When she has a _____, she has

2

to stay home.

Last month, Tara had _____. She felt terrible and called in sick for three

3

days. Then two of her children got sick. She _____ home for two more

4

days.

Tara's manager _____. There is a lot of work. Tara doesn't want

5

_____.

6

B Match the pictures with the excuses. Use the sentences in the box.

I feel terrible. I have a cold.	~~I missed the bus.~~
My child has a fever.	I'm tired today.

1. _I missed the bus._

2. _____

3. _____

4. _____

A Read the chart. Then add your own information.

Ali and Fatima

Arnold

Yesterday at...	Ali and Fatima	Arnold	My information
2 p.m.	eat lunch	read a book	
6 p.m.	shop for food	make dinner	
8 p.m.	do laundry	jog	
10 p.m.	study	read his email	

B Look at the chart in A. Complete the sentences. Use the past continuous.

1. Ali and Fatima _____*were shopping for food*_____ at 6 p.m.

2. They _____ at 2 p.m.

3. Arnold _____ at 8 p.m.

4. Ali and Fatima _____ at 10 p.m.

5. Arnold _____ at 6 p.m.

6. He _____ at 10 p.m.

C Write about yourself. Use your information from the chart in A. Use the past continuous.

1. _____

2. _____

3. _____

4. _____

D **Complete the answers. Use the past continuous.**

1. **A:** Was she sleeping at 9:30?

   B: Yes, _she was sleeping_ at 9:30.

2. **A:** Were they making coffee in the morning?

   B: No, _____ in the morning.

3. **A:** Was he working on the computer?

   B: No, _____ on the computer.

4. **A:** Were you exercising at 7 a.m.?

   B: Yes, _____ at 7 a.m.

E **Match the questions with the answers.**

_c_ 1. Was she driving her car at 9 p.m.?

____ 2. What was he doing at 5 p.m.?

____ 3. Was Steve writing an email?

____ 4. What was Jin doing at 7 a.m.?

____ 5. Were they watching TV yesterday afternoon?

____ 6. What were Elena and Fernando doing at 3 p.m.?

a. Yes, he was.

b. He was studying.

c. No, she wasn't.

d. They were eating.

e. No, they weren't.

f. She was shopping for food.

F **Grammar Boost** **Complete the sentences. Use the present continuous or the past continuous.**

1. I _____am writing_____ an email to my teacher now. (write)

2. What _____were_____ you _____doing_____ at the park yesterday? (do)

3. Julie _____ for her test right now. (study)

4. _____ she _____ to work yesterday at 7:30 a.m.? (drive)

5. Please don't talk. We _____ a math test. (take)

6. What _____ she _____ at 8:30 last night? (do)

7. Right now I _____ breakfast. (eat)

8. Where _____ they _____ last night? (go)

A Complete the conversation. Use the words in the box.

May I take	~~can I help you~~	This is
speak to Mr. Gonzalez	give him the message	isn't in

Takeshi: Good morning, Good Food Restaurant.

How _can I help you_____?
1

Carlos: Hello. May I _____, please?
2

Takeshi: I'm sorry. He _____ today.
3

_____ a message?
4

Carlos: Yes. _____ Carlos Hernandez,
5

his accountant. Can you ask Mr. Gonzalez to call me, please? My number

is 555-4724.

Takeshi: OK. I'll _____ tomorrow.
6

Carlos: Thank you. Goodbye.

B Look at the conversation in A. Complete the telephone message.

While you were out...

For:

From:

Message

C **Real-life math** Circle *a* or *b*.

Janet uses a phone card to make long distance calls to her family in Russia.
She can talk for 5 hours and spend $27.00. How much does it cost Janet to
call Russia for 1 hour?

a. $13.50

b. $5.40

A Read the article.

Retirement Communities

Many Americans move to retirement[1] communities when they get older. A retirement community is a place for seniors to live, and it offers many different services. Counselors give seniors advice, and nurses care for their health. At social events, seniors can have fun and meet new people.

In retirement communities, there are usually volunteers. In their free time, volunteers help the seniors. For example, they go for walks with the seniors, do housework for them, or help them pay bills.

In the United States, there are many retirement communities. Seniors are living longer now, and they need nice places to live. In the early 1900s, the life expectancy[2] was 51 years old for women and 48 years old for men. Now the life expectancy for women is 80 and 74 for men.

Seniors in retirement communities want a comfortable life. The services and volunteers help the seniors a lot. Life in these communities can be cheerful and busy.

[1] retirement: when someone doesn't work anymore
[2] life expectancy: the average time a people live.

B Mark the sentences T (true) or F (false).

_F_ 1. A retirement community does not offer services to seniors.

____ 2. Volunteers don't work with seniors in retirement communities.

____ 3. There aren't a lot of retirement communities in the U.S.

____ 4. Americans live longer now.

____ 5. The life expectancy for men was 48 in the early 1900s.

A Complete the sentences. Use the words in the box.

| local service | make a call | ~~previous charges~~ | total due | cell phone |

1. The p__ r__ e__ v__ i__ o__ u__ s__ c__ h__ a__ r__ g__ e__ s

    (1 = i, 2 = s, 3 = g)

    on my phone bill were $29.70.

2. I never use my ___ ___ ___ ___ ___ ___ in the

    (4, 5, 6)

    movie theater.

3. I don't use my ___ ___ ___ ___ ___ ___ ___ ___ ___ ___

    (7, 8)

    to make international calls.

4. I need to ___ ___ ___ ___ ___ ___ ___ to my doctor to

    (9, 10, 11)

    make an appointment.

5. The ___ ___ ___ ___ ___ ___ ___ ___ for my phone bill this month

    (12, 13, 14)

    is $43.80.

B Look at the picture. Then answer the question. Use the code in A.

What is he doing?

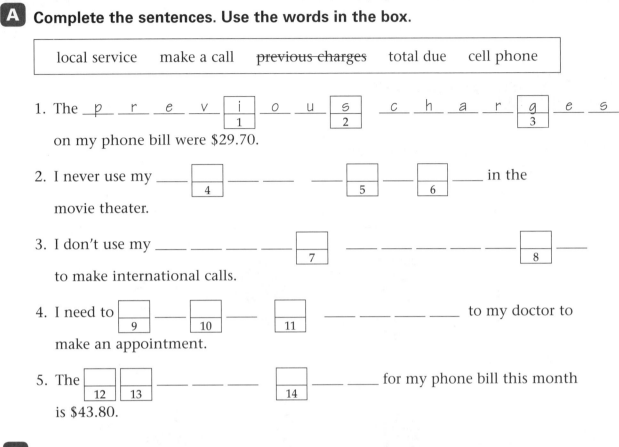

___ ___ i s ___ ___ i g ___
5   4   1 2   9 11 10 1 6 3   11

___ ___ ___ g ___ i s ___ ___ ___ ___ ___ ___ ___ ___ ___ ___ .
7 13 6 3   14 1 2   12 11 6 8 4   8 11 7 7

UNIT 7

What's for Dinner?

LESSON 1 **Vocabulary**

A **Look at the pictures. Match the words with the pictures. Use the words in the box.**

| jar   bunch   carton   box   can   bottle   bag   ~~package~~ |

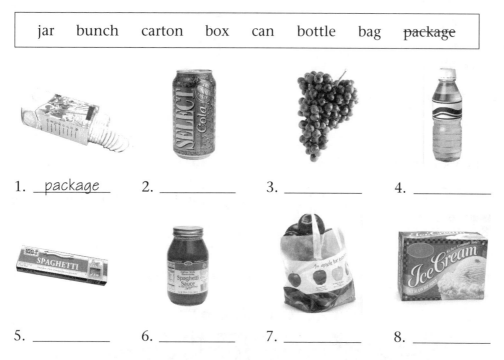

1. __package__   2. _____   3. _____   4. _____

5. _____   6. _____   7. _____   8. _____

B **Complete the conversation. Use the words in A.**

Dina: Hi, Cesar. Would you like me to cook that ____box____ of spaghetti for dinner?
1

Cesar: That's a good idea. I'll open a _____ of spaghetti sauce for you. What
2
about a drink?

Dina: That would be nice. Can I have a _____ of water?
3

Cesar: Sure. I'll have a _____ of soda. What about that _____ of grapes?
4   5
Should we have them, too?

Dina: OK. We have a _____ of ice cream. Maybe we can have some after dinner.
6

Cesar: Well, I shouldn't eat any dessert tonight. I had some earlier.

A **Complete the paragraph. Use the words in the box.**

prices	unit prices	cheap	a problem
a lot of coupons	at saving money	~~like to spend a lot~~	supermarket advertisements

Lisa and Adam don't _____ like to spend a lot _____ of money on food.

1

How do they save money? First, they read the _____

2

and compare _____ at home. At the supermarket,

3

they check the _____ and buy store brands. They

4

also use _____.

5

Lisa and Adam are good _____ at the

6

supermarket, but sometimes they want a special kind of food, like ice cream.

This isn't _____. They just buy the

7

_____ brand!

8

B **Look at the flyers. Then answer the questions. Use complete sentences.**

1. Which juice is a better buy, one gallon for $4.00 or a half gallon for 2.50?

   One gallon for $4.00 is a better buy.

2. Which cheese is a better buy, ten ounces for $3.95 or five ounces for $1.90?

   _____

3. Which ice cream is a better buy, two pints for $6.00 or one pint for $2.75?

   _____

4. Which bunch of grapes is a better buy, two bunches for $2.99 or one bunch for $1.75?

   _____

A Look at the pictures. Circle the count nouns and underline the noncount nouns.

1. (carrots)

2. butter

3. potatoes

4. salt

5. water

6. mushrooms

B Check (✓) *How many* or *How much*. Then complete the questions.

	How many	*How much*	Questions
1. tomatoes	✓		How many tomatoes _____ do you have?
2. soda			_____ do you have?
3. flour			_____ do you have?
4. bananas			_____ do you have?

C Complete the questions. Use *How many* or *How much*.

1. **A:** How much _____ cheese do you want?

   B: I want eight ounces of cheese, please.

2. **A:** _____ oranges does she eat every day?

   B: She eats two oranges every day.

3. **A:** _____ cartons of milk do they have?

   B: They have two cartons of milk.

4. **A:** _____ juice does he drink a day?

   B: He drinks eight ounces of juice a day.

D **Unscramble the sentences.**

1. need / some / They / milk

   <u>They need some milk.</u>

2. doesn't / tomatoes / any / She / have

   _____

3. some / salt / There's / in the soup

   _____

4. He / any / cheese / eat / doesn't

   _____

5. want / oil / some / We

   _____

E 🚀 **Grammar Boost** **Complete the conversations. Use** *a, an, any,*
some, how many, or *how much.*

1. **A:** Did you buy _____ some _____ milk?

   B: Yes, I did. There's _____ carton of
   milk in the refrigerator.

   A: Great! Can I have _____ milk for
   my coffee?

2. **A:** I'd like _____ egg and
   _____ bread for breakfast, please.

   B: I'm sorry. _____ eggs do you want?
   Do you want _____ jam, too?

   A: I want one egg, but I don't want
   _____ jam.

3. **A:** _____ olive oil do we have?

   B: We don't have _____ olive oil.

   A: Can you please buy _____
   olive oil at the supermarket?

4. **A:** Are there _____ apples in the refrigerator?

   B: Yes, there are. _____ do you want?

A **Put the sentences in the conversation in the correct order.**

_____	**Keiko:**	OK, aisle 3. Thank you. Oh, and the sausages?
_____	**Clerk:**	The tuna is in aisle 3, next to the soup.
_____	**Clerk:**	Sausages? You can find them in the meat section.
_____	**Keiko:**	That's everything I need. Thanks a lot.
_1_	**Keiko:**	Excuse me. Where's the tuna, please?
_____	**Clerk:**	You're welcome.

B **Where can you find these items? Match the food with the supermarket sections.**

1 fruit and vegetables

2 sausages and chicken

3 cookies and bread

4 butter and milk

5 soup and tuna

| _____ baked goods | _____ dairy | _____ canned goods |
| _1_ produce | _____ meat | |

C **Real-life math** **Circle a or b.**

Ali has $2.75 in his wallet. He wants to buy some sugar. One pound of sugar is $0.99. How much sugar can Ali buy?

a. Ali can buy 2 pounds of sugar.

b. Ali can buy 3 pounds of sugar.

A Read the article.

A Healthy Diet for a Busy Lifestyle

Many people don't eat the right food because they are busy. They think it takes a lot of time to have a healthy diet, but that's not always true. Many healthy foods are quick and easy to prepare.

For example, put some cheese, tomatoes, and cold chicken on whole-grain bread. To add some calcium, eat some yogurt. This healthy lunch is ready in minutes.

Fruit and vegetables are also easy to eat. Take a bag of grapes, oranges, or apples to work or school. Cut some carrots and eat them. Don't forget, vegetable soup is always great on a cool day.

It's important to drink the right things too. Soda has a lot of sugar and calories, and drinking too many cups of coffee is not healthy. Drink milk, juice, or water. Many doctors want people to drink eight cups of water every day!

On busy days, people can have a healthy diet. It might be easy to open a bag of potato chips but they are not healthy. Nuts are healthier than potato chips, and it's also easy to open a package of nuts! ■

B Look at A. Mark the sentences T (true) or F (false). Change the false sentences. Make them true.

  _F_   1. It *doesn't* ~~takes~~ a lot of time to eat healthy food.

  ____   2. Yogurt doesn't have calcium.

  ____   3. Grapes, oranges, and apples can be easy to eat.

  ____   4. Potato chips are healthier than nuts.

  ____   5. Busy people can have a healthy diet.

C Read the nutrition label. Write the questions.

1. _How many servings are in a box?_

   There are eight servings in a box.

2. _____

   One serving is two ounces.

3. _____

   There are 200 calories in one serving.

4. _____

   There are ten calories from fat in one serving.

Nutrition Facts		
Servings per box: 8		
Serving size: 2 oz		
Amount per serving		
Calories per serving:		200
Calories from fat:		10
		% Daily Value
Total fat 1g		2%
Saturated fat 0g		0%
Trans fat 0g		
Cholesterol 0mg		0%

A Circle the containers, weights, and measurements in the puzzle.

| quart | bunch | can | pint | pound | box | ~~ounces~~ | carton | package | bag |

B	U	N	C	H	Y	J	N	H	P	I	N	T
W	E	J	N	V	U	T	R	O	Y	Q	Z	M
S	X	Z	V	F	A	W	A	U	Q	B	A	G
N	N	S	K	J	U	I	S	N	B	T	D	W
C	N	L	K	U	P	A	T	C	O	G	E	Q
P	A	C	K	A	G	E	O	E	F	H	K	U
R	J	A	H	Y	Z	M	Q	S	H	Y	D	A
T	V	R	T	E	I	I	T	M	W	N	X	R
O	P	T	Y	U	V	Z	N	N	O	M	Y	T
N	N	O	R	E	V	O	Z	N	D	W	C	T
C	W	N	A	P	O	U	N	D	W	X	A	Y
A	S	B	B	L	R	D	N	T	X	Z	N	T
J	N	A	Q	M	S	S	B	O	X	X	Y	Y

B Complete the chart. Use the words in the box.

a quart of juice	a bunch of bananas	~~16 ounces of chicken~~	a pint of ice cream
a pound of sausages	a box of cookies	a can of soda	a carton of milk
a package of bread	a bag of apples		

Meat	16 ounces of chicken
Dairy	
Drinks	
Produce	
Baked Goods	

Stay Safe and Well

Vocabulary

A **Complete the sentences. Use the words in the box.**

antihistamine	antacid	~~cough syrup~~
antibiotic ointment	eardrops	pain reliever

1. Rasha is coughing a lot. Can she have some _____cough syrup_____?

2. Naomi is allergic to cats. Please give her an _____.

3. I have a bad headache. Do you have any _____?

4. Rico ate spicy food and has heartburn now. He wants
   to take an _____.

5. Antonia has an earache. She needs _____.

6. You should use some _____ for the cut on your hand.

B **Look at the picture. Match the sentences with the numbers.**

_____ Alex has a rash.   _____ Carlos has a fever.

_1_ Dan's ankle is swollen.   _____ Lisa is nauseous and dizzy.

_____ Midori is sneezing and has a runny nose.   _____ Julie has a cough.

A Look at the pictures. Complete the paragraphs. Use the words in the box.

| had a backache | gave him a filling | to the chiropractor |
| a~~ bad toothache~~ | made an appointment | have to rest |

Nadim had a terrible day yesterday. In the morning, he woke up with

_____a bad toothache_____. He called in sick, and then he _____
         1   2

to see the dentist. At the appointment, the dentist _____.
                                                   3

In the afternoon, Nadim hurt his back. He _____. He went
                                                4

_____. The chiropractor said, "You _____ for
           5   6
a few days."

That night, Nadim went to bed and tried to forget about his day.

B Complete the conversation. Use the words in the box.

| see the pediatrician | ~~make an appointment~~ | Could you make |
| That's good | the problem | about 11:30 |

A: Good morning. I need to ___make an appointment___ for my son. He needs
                                   1

    to _____.
              2

B: What's _____?
             3

A: Well, he has a terrible cough, and he has a fever.

B: How _____ this morning?
              4

A: My son is very sick. _____ it earlier?
                       5

B: How about 9:30?

A: _____. Thank you very much!
           6

A Complete the sentences. Use the past continuous and simple past.

1. Mei _____was driving_____ when she _____had_____ the accident. (drive, have)

2. James _____ with his children when he _____ his leg. (play, break)

3. They _____ TV when they _____ the phone call. (watch, get)

4. I _____ a book when the baby _____ his hand. (read, hurt)

5. We _____ dinner when the package _____. (have, arrive)

6. He _____ lunch when he _____ his finger. (cook, cut)

B Write sentences. Use the past continuous and simple past.

1. Nancy / watch TV / when / fall asleep

   Nancy was watching TV when she fell asleep.

2. The children / play soccer / when / see / an accident

   _____

3. Binita / study / when / get / a headache

   _____

4. Natasha and Boris / ski / when / fall in love

   _____

5. He / clean / when / hurt / his back

   _____

C Complete the sentences. Use the past continuous and your own ideas.

My husband was cooking when I got home yesterday.

1. Her kids _____ when I got home yesterday.

2. We _____ when the teacher arrived.

3. She _____ when she burned her hand.

4. His son _____ when I got up this morning.

D Look at the pictures. Complete the conversations. Use the words in the box.

had an	was playing	his arm
~~burned~~	was painting	was cooking

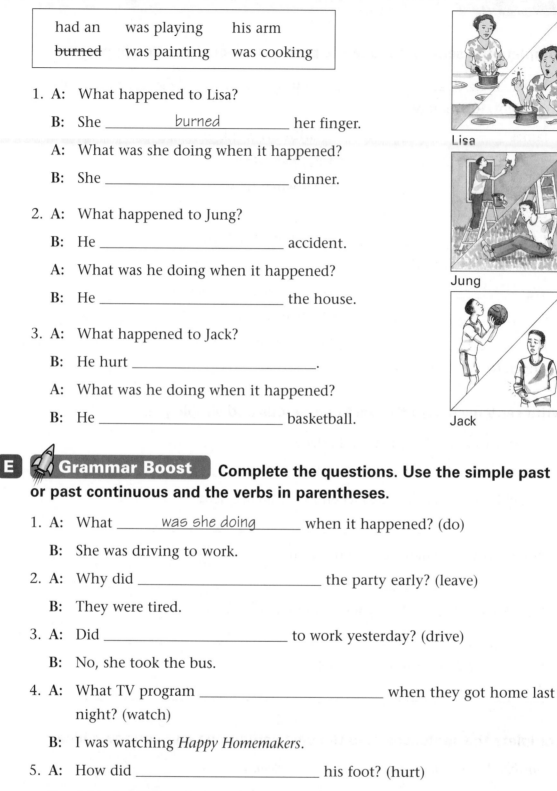

Lisa

Jung

Jack

1. **A:** What happened to Lisa?

   B: She _____ burned _____ her finger.

   A: What was she doing when it happened?

   B: She _____ dinner.

2. **A:** What happened to Jung?

   B: He _____ accident.

   A: What was he doing when it happened?

   B: He _____ the house.

3. **A:** What happened to Jack?

   B: He hurt _____.

   A: What was he doing when it happened?

   B: He _____ basketball.

E 🚀 Grammar Boost   Complete the questions. Use the simple past or past continuous and the verbs in parentheses.

1. **A:** What _____ was she doing _____ when it happened? (do)

   B: She was driving to work.

2. **A:** Why did _____ the party early? (leave)

   B: They were tired.

3. **A:** Did _____ to work yesterday? (drive)

   B: No, she took the bus.

4. **A:** What TV program _____ when they got home last night? (watch)

   B: I was watching *Happy Homemakers*.

5. **A:** How did _____ his foot? (hurt)

   B: A big box fell on it.

A Complete the conversation. Use the words in the box.

How often	~~your prescription~~	refill the prescription
times a day	for ten days	take more than

Dr. Zakari: OK, Lina. Here is _____your prescription_____.

1

Lina: _____ should I take the pills?

2

Dr. Zakari: Three _____. Take one pill every eight hours.

3

Don't _____ three pills a day.

4

Lina: For how long?

Dr. Zakari: Take them _____. Then come back to see me. I might

5

want you to _____.

6

Lina: Thank you, Dr. Zakari.

B Read the prescription label. Mark the sentences T (true) or F (false).

_F_ 1. This prescription is for Dr. Chow.

____ 2. This prescription is for shoulder pain.

____ 3. Ali should eat food when he takes
a pill.

____ 4. It's OK to take 10 pills a day.

____ 5. Ali can refill the prescription until
December 2010.

> WT's Parmacy
> Ali Hala
> 822 Reddy Street
> Palo Alto, CA 94306
>
> Take 1 pill by mouth 2 times a day
> for shoulder pain. Take with meals.
> No more than 8 pills every 24 hours.
>
> **Refill: 2 Before 05/12/10**
> Prescription from: Dr. Chow

C **Real-life math** Circle *a* or *b*.

1. Lisa has some new medication. The bottle has 40 pills. She also needs to refill it
three times. How many pills will she take in total?
a. 120 pills
b. 160 pills

2. Every day, Wen took one pill after breakfast and one pill after dinner. After 30
days, the bottle was empty. How many pills did Wen take?
a. 60 pills
b. 30 pills

A Read the article.

Accidents on the Job

Sometimes there are accidents in the workplace. What should you do when there is an accident at work? Here are three important rules to follow:

1. **Help injured employees immediately.** Get the first-aid kit, and use the supplies. In a serious emergency, call a doctor or emergency services.

2. **Write down all important information.** Who was injured? When and where did the accident happen? How did the accident happen?

3. **Complete an accident report for your supervisor.** Your supervisor has to know about the accident. It's important that the right people have all the forms they need. This helps the injured person get good medical treatment[1] now and in the future.

For accidents at work, know what to do before they happen. Find the first-aid kit, and check the supplies. Write down emergency telephone numbers. In the future, you will be ready and can help co-workers or yourself.

[1] medical treatment: help for an injured person

B Mark the sentences T (true) or F (false).

__T__ 1. After an accident, the first step is to help any injured people.

_____ 2. You always have to call emergency services when there's an accident.

_____ 3. The supervisor needs to know about accidents at work.

_____ 4. Find the first-aid kit after an accident.

_____ 5. An accident report doesn't help an injured person.

C Look at the first-aid supplies. Check (✓) the supplies you see.

__✓__ bandages   _____ gloves

_____ thermometer   _____ antibiotic ointment

_____ scissors   _____ antiseptic wipes

A Complete the paragraph. Use the words in the box.

allergic	antihistamine	swollen	injured	fever
sneezing	~~antiseptic~~	runny	pain	bandage

The nurse at our company was very busy yesterday. First, Mr. Harris cut his finger.

The nurse cleaned it with an ____antiseptic____ wipe and put a _____ on it.
                                    4-down   3-down

Then Ms. Jones came in. She had a _____ nose and was _____
                                              2-down   9-across

a lot. Ms. Jones was probably _____ to something, so the nurse gave her an
                                        6-across

_____. Then Mr. Wilson came in. He felt hot. He had a _____
        4-across   8-across

and a headache. The nurse gave him a _____ reliever. Finally, Mr. Dodd came
                                                1-down

in. He _____ his ankle when he fell on the stairs. It was _____, so
          5-down   7-across

the nurse told him to rest. What a busy day!

B Write the words in the puzzle. Use the information in A.

Money Matters

LESSON 1 Vocabulary

A Look at the bank statement. Complete the sentences. Use the words in the box.

| bank statement | credit card bill | ATM card |
| personal check | current balance | savings account |

1. Every month Luisa gets a _____bank statement_____ for her checking account.

2. Her _____ for this month is $2,000.50.

3. Luisa wrote a _____ to Oakwood Apartments.

4. Luisa used her _____ to withdraw $20.00.

5. Luisa transferred $100 to her _____.

6. Luisa paid $250.50 for her _____.

◀ STATE BANK   *Page 1 of 3*

Monthly statement

CHECKING ACCOUNT	CURRENT BALANCE
9876543	$2,000.50

DATE	TRANSACTION	AMOUNT
2/01	Oakwood Apt. rent—check #167	800.00
2/10	Internet payment— Star Energy	150.00
2/16	Deposit	500.00
2/18	Withdrawal—ATM	20.00
2/20	Transfer—savings account	100.00
2/20	Quest Credit— check #168	250.50

B Complete the sentences. Use the words in the box.

| your PIN | enter the amount | remove your |
| insert your ATM | take your cash | insert the deposit |

1. First, _____insert your ATM_____ card for service.

2. Next, enter _____.

3. For a deposit, _____ envelope.

4. For cash, first _____ you want to withdraw and press *Enter*.

5. Then _____ from the ATM.

6. Finally, don't forget to _____ ATM card before you go.

A Complete the paragraph. Use the words in the box.

| has a special offer | total budget | a great bargain | have picnics | cost $35 |
| compare the prices | a picnic table | he goes home | makes a list | ~~fix up~~ |

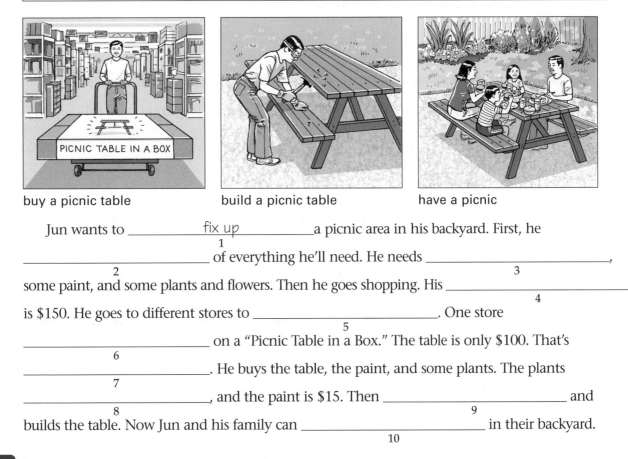

buy a picnic table   build a picnic table   have a picnic

Jun wants to _____fix up_____ a picnic area in his backyard. First, he
1
_____ of everything he'll need. He needs _____,
2   3
some paint, and some plants and flowers. Then he goes shopping. His _____
4
is $150. He goes to different stores to _____. One store
5
_____ on a "Picnic Table in a Box." The table is only $100. That's
6
_____. He buys the table, the paint, and some plants. The plants
7
_____, and the paint is $15. Then _____ and
8   9
builds the table. Now Jun and his family can _____ in their backyard.
10

B Read the paragraph. Complete the chart.

Gabriela wants to fix up her new office, but she doesn't have a lot of money. She needs
a file cabinet, a new computer desk, a comfortable chair, and a picture for the wall. She
can spend $275. A co-worker wants to sell his file cabinet for $75. There's a desk on sale for
$80 at a store near Gabriela's house. She also saw a chair in a newspaper flyer. It costs $65.
Gabriela still has money for a picture. How much money can she spend on the picture?

Gabriela's new office	Amount
file cabinet	$75
computer desk	
comfortable chair	
picture for the wall	
Total budget: $275	

A Match the parts of the sentences.

_d_ 1. Joe bought some stamps to   a. she wanted to exercise.

_____ 2. Sasha bought eardrops because   b. buy a pain reliever.

_____ 3. Paula went to the park because   c. she had an earache.

_____ 4. Jeff went to the pharmacy to   d. mail some letters.

B Complete the sentences. Write *it, they,* or *X*. (*X* = nothing)

1. Pablo wrote a personal check to _____X_____ pay his credit card bill.

2. The photocopier broke because _____ was old.

3. Ana and Rita got their GED certificates because _____ wanted better jobs.

4. Adam needs more work experience to _____ apply for that job.

5. Yoshi likes his apartment because _____ is in a safe neighborhood.

6. Carol bought three packages of cookies because _____ were on sale.

C Answer the questions. Use *to* or *because* and the words in parentheses.

to + verb

1. A: Why did Yasmin go to the hospital? (visit her mother)

   B: _She went to the hospital to visit her mother._____

2. A: Why did Mario go to the bank? (deposit a check)

   B: _____

3. A: Why did Sue go to the library? (return some books)

   B: _____

because

4. A: Why did Mario go to the ATM? (needed some cash)

   B: _____

5. A: Why did James go to the baseball game? (had tickets)

   B: _____

6. A: Why did Oko and Paul go to the supermarket? (wanted some sugar)

   B: _____

D **Look at the pictures. Compete the sentences. Use the words in the box.**

| to refill a prescription | wanted some books |
| ~~wanted a bachelor's degree~~ | to withdraw some money |

1. Franco went to school because he

   <u>wanted a bachelor's</u>

   <u>degree</u>   .

3. Tom went to the pharmacy

   _____ .

2. Wendy went to the bank

   _____

   _____ .

4. Min went to the library because she

   _____

   _____ .

E 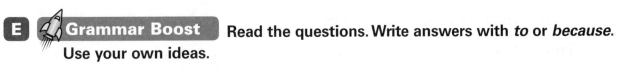 **Grammar Boost** **Read the questions. Write answers with *to* or *because*. Use your own ideas.**

1. Why do people use ATM cards?

   They use ATM cards _____

   _____

2. Why do people go to home-improvement stores?

   They go to home-improvement stores _____

   _____

3. Why do people study English?

   They study English _____

   _____

> **Need help?**
>
> **Answer ideas**
> *to withdraw cash*
> *to fix up their houses*
> *to get a better job*

A Put the conversation in the correct order.

_____ **Customer:** Because it's too big. I need a smaller one. Here's my receipt.

_____ **Customer:** I'd like to exchange it, please.

__1__ **Customer:** Good morning. I would like to return this shirt.

_____ **Clerk:** Would you like a refund, or do you want to exchange the shirt?

_____ **Clerk:** OK. Why are you returning it?

B Complete the conversation. Use the sentences in the box.

You can't get a refund without a receipt.	Because I don't like the color.
I'll exchange it for a different color.	Why are you returning it?
~~I'd like to return this sweater.~~	I don't have it.

Jane: Excuse me. _I'd like to return this sweater._
1

Clerk: That's fine. _____
2

Jane: _____
3

Clerk: OK. Do you have your receipt?

Jane: Yes, I think so. Oh, no! _____
4

Clerk: I'm sorry. _____ Would you like to
5
exchange it?

Jane: OK. _____
6

C 🖩 **Real-life math** Circle *a* or *b*.

Luis went to the Men's Wear store and bought two shirts. They cost $25.95 each. He also bought a tie for $13.00. The next day, he returned one shirt and got a refund. Then he bought another tie. How much money did Luis spend?

a. $51.95   b. $10.95

A Read the article.

Lose a Credit Card? What to Do

Did you lose your credit card? Did someone take your card? If yes, this is what you should do:

1. *Call the credit card company immediately.* Explain what happened. They will cancel your card. Then no one can buy things with it. Federal law says that credit card companies cannot make you pay more than $50 for charges on a lost card, but you need to report the problem immediately.

2. *Send a letter to the credit card company.* Write about what happened to your credit card. Did someone buy things with your card? Tell the company about that, too. List purchases and amounts. Include the name of the person you spoke with on the phone.

3. *Check your credit card bill.* Look at your next credit card bill carefully. Are there problems? Call the credit card company again and write another letter.

The credit card company will usually send you a new card quickly. Take good care of the new card and keep the credit card company's phone number in a safe place. Then it will be easier to report any problems in the future.

B Answer the questions.

1. When should you report a missing credit card?

   You should report a missing credit card immediately.

2. What is the first thing you should do after you lose a credit card?

   _____

3. What should you do after you call the credit card company?

   _____

4. What should you do with your next credit card bill?

   _____

5. Where should you keep the credit card company's phone number?

   _____

A Circle the words in the puzzle.

return	deposit	~~balance~~	bank statement
check	budget	credit card	savings account

```
D  E  P  O  S  I  T  F  C  A  B  C  O  R  H
T  Z  H  P  A  W  N  E  N  U  G  W  D  B  M
I  N  M  C  X  L  B  E  R  E  T  U  R  N  P
V  Y  U  R  G  H  U  M  Q  A  R  D  O  S  K
U  K  X  E  B  N  D  E  C  M  R  V  V  S  L
P  T  M  D  C  I  G  T  X  C  H  E  C  K  D
Q  D  E  I  E  C  E  A  C  L  S  K  R  B  T
U  C  E  T  B  O  T  A  T  J  I  F  E  P  L
P  S  K  C  O  U  I  S  O  M  X  G  B  W  D
M  P  B  A  N  K  S  T  A  T  E  M  E  N  T
L  V  C  R  E  H  D  N  J  N  H  K  Q  J  D
W  D  F  D  I  F  B  A  W  O  I  P  N  E  M
R  Y  M  B  H  N  D  J  Y  F  H  T  P  S  X
S  A  V  I  N  G  S  A  C  C  O  U  N  T  U
B  A  L  A  N  C  E  W  R  K  A  N  A  X  Y
```

B Complete the sentences. Use the words in A.

1. Fernando always knows the current _____balance_____ in his checking account.

2. Gabriela has $5,000 in her _____.

3. Alan got a new shirt from his sister, but it's too small. He wants to _____ it.

4. Every month we _____ $500 in our checking account.

5. Julio has personal checks, an ATM card, and one _____.

6. Ali always checks his _____ carefully.

7. Sara has to write a _____ for her rent every month.

8. Sue wants to fix up her bathroom. Her _____ is $200.

Steps to Citizenship

LESSON 1 **Vocabulary**

A **Match the words with the pictures.**

What is the 4th of July?

_____ take an oath of allegiance

_____ take a citizenship test

_____ get a passport

_____ fill out an application for naturalization

___1___ get a permanent resident card

B **Complete the chart. Use the words in the box.**

| ~~Congress~~ | governor | city council members | president | U.S. representative |
| U.S. senator | vice president | lieutenant governor | mayor | |

Federal Government	State Government	Local Government
Congress		

A **Complete the paragraph. Use the words in the box.**

decided to do	doesn't have enough	to raise money	help clean the park
~~went to a meeting~~	Grant Park is dirty	had an idea	people at the meeting

David and Angela live in a small town. One evening, they ___went to a meeting___

　　　　　　　　　　　　　　　　　　　　　　　　　　　　　　　　　　　1

of their neighborhood association. The _____ discussed many

　　　　　　　　　　　　　　　　　　　　　2

community issues. For example, one problem was that _____. The

　　　　　　　　　　　　　　　　　　　　　　　　　　　　　3

town _____ money to clean it. Angela _____.

　　　　　　　4　　　　　　　　　　　　　　　　　　　　　　　　　　5

She said, "Let's ask volunteers from the neighborhood to help." At the meeting they

_____ two things:

　　　　6

　1. have a book sale _____ for the park,

　　　　　　　　　　　　　7

　2. ask people in the neighborhood to _____.

　　　　　　　　　　　　　　　　　　　8

The plan worked. Now the park is clean, and everyone in the neighborhood can use it.

B **Read the flyer. Answer the questions. Use complete sentences.**

1. What's happening on June 10th?

　There will be a book sale.

2. What's the date for the park cleanup?

　_____

3. What time does it start?

　_____

4. Do the volunteers need to buy lunch?

　_____

5. Who do you call for more information?

　_____

> **Grant Street Park Cleanup Project!**
>
> *Book Sale to raise money
> Date: Saturday, June 10th
> Time: 10 a.m. to 4 p.m.
> Place: Grant Street School
>
> *Park cleanup day
> We will provide lunch for everyone!
> Date: Saturday, June 17th
> Time: 10 a.m. to 5 p.m.
> ❀ ❀ ❀
> For more information call:
> Angela Banks (215) 555-4392

A Look at the train rules. Complete the sentences with *must* or *must not*.

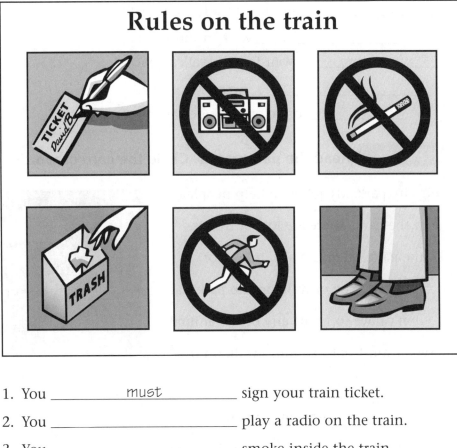

Rules on the train

1. You _____ *must* _____ sign your train ticket.

2. You _____ play a radio on the train.

3. You _____ smoke inside the train.

4. You _____ throw away trash.

5. You _____ run in the aisles.

6. You _____ wear shoes on the train.

B Mark the sentences T (true) or F (false). Change the false sentences. Make them true.

Rules on the airplane
Arrive on time.
Fasten your seat belt.
Don't smoke in the bathroom.
No cell phones.
Don't put your feet in the aisle.

_F_ 1. You must ^ *not* use a cell phone.

_____ 2. You must fasten your seat belt.

_____ 3. You must not arrive on time.

_____ 4. You must not smoke in the bathroom.

_____ 5. You must put your feet in the aisle.

C **Complete the sentences. Use _must_ or _must not_.**

1. In a restaurant, you _____ _must_ _____ pay for your food.

   You _____ run.

2. On a bus, you _____ play your radio too loud.

   You _____ stand behind the yellow line.

3. Pedestrians _____ walk in the street.

   They _____ wait for the walk signal.

4. In a car, you _____ wear a seat belt.

   You _____ drive on the sidewalk.

D **Grammar Boost**   **Read the paragraphs. Circle the correct words.**

I work in a big city park. My job is to help people

enjoy their time in the park. There are lots of things

people can do in the park. There are also rules. For

example, you ((can) / must) jog or walk on the park trails.
                  1

You (shouldn't / don't have to) hurt any of the animals
         2

in the park, and you (must not / should) walk on the
                          3

flowers.

The park closes at 11 p.m. every day, so you

(have to / must not) come into the park after that time.
         4

Sometimes, people ask me, "(Can / Must) I jog in the park
                              5

after 9 p.m.?" I say, "Well, you (can / must), but I don't
                                        6

think you (should / have to). It (might not / must not)
               7   8

be safe." I really like to help people, so I like my job a lot!

A **Complete the conversation. Use the words in the box.**

photo ID	take care of it	photo is
~~Good morning~~	I see	it is

Security officer: _____ Good morning _____.
1

May _____ your
2

_____, please?
3

Mario: Sure. Here _____.
4

Security officer: Did you know that your

_____ too old?
5

Mario: No, I'm sorry. I'll

_____
6

right away.

Security officer: OK. Have a good day.

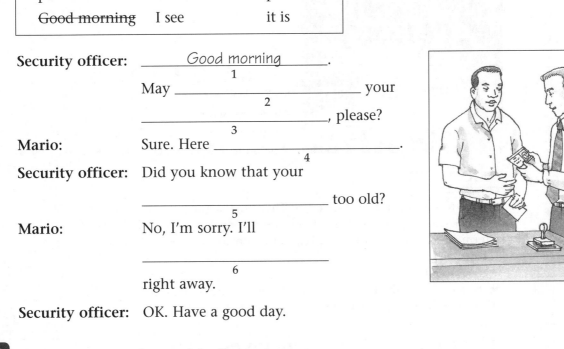

B **Match the questions with the answers.**

__e__ 1. May I see your license and
registration, please?

____ 2. Did you know that your right
taillight is broken?

____ 3. May I see your train pass?

____ 4. You must not speed on this street.

____ 5. Your passport has no signature.

a. No, I didn't. I'll take care of it
right away.

b. I'm sorry, officer. I'll slow down.

c. I don't have one. It expired last week.

d. I'll sign it right now.

e. Sure officer. Here they are.

C **Complete the sentences. Circle the correct words.**

1. You (must /(should)) wear a sweater. It is cold outside.

2. You (must not / should not) go over the speed limit.

3. They (must / should) wear a seatbelt.

4. You (must / should) check your car engine regularly.

A **Read about the U.S. Congress.**

The U.S. Congress

There are two parts of the U.S. Congress: the Senate and the House of Representatives. What's the difference between these two parts?

The Senate

There are 100 senators in the Senate. There are two senators for each of the 50 states. Senators are elected, and being a senator is a full-time job. The job is for a term of six years. After this six-year term, senators can be reelected[1]. To be a senator, you must:
★ be 30 years old,
★ be a citizen of the United States for at least nine years, and
★ be a resident of the state where you're elected.

The House of Representatives

There are 435 representatives in the House of Representatives. Representatives are elected, and this is a full-time job for them, too. The job is for a term of two years. After this two-year term, representatives can be reelected. The number of representatives is different for each state. States with large populations have more representatives than states with small populations. To be a representative, you must:
★ be 25 years old,
★ be a citizen of the United States for at least seven years, and
★ be a resident of the state where you're elected.

[1] reelected: elected again

B **Mark the sentences T (true) or F (false).**

___T___ 1. There are 100 senators in the Senate.

_____ 2. There are only 100 representatives in the House of Representatives.

_____ 3. You must be 25 years old to be a senator.

_____ 4. The president chooses senators and representatives.

_____ 5. Senators and representatives can be reelected.

_____ 6. You don't have to be a U.S. citizen to be in Congress.

A **Complete the sentences. Use the words in the box.**

speeding	application	signature	test	council
~~vice~~	federal	oath	Senate	

1. Who is the _____vice_____ president of the United States?

2. To become a citizen, you must take an _____ of allegiance.

3. Did you complete your _____ for naturalization?

4. The mayor and city _____ members meet every month.

5. There is no _____ on your passport. You must sign it.

6. Did you pass the citizenship _____?

7. Slow down! You're really _____!

8. The U.S. Congress has two parts: the _____ and the House of Representatives.

9. Congress is part of the _____ government.

B **Complete the puzzle. Use the words in A.**

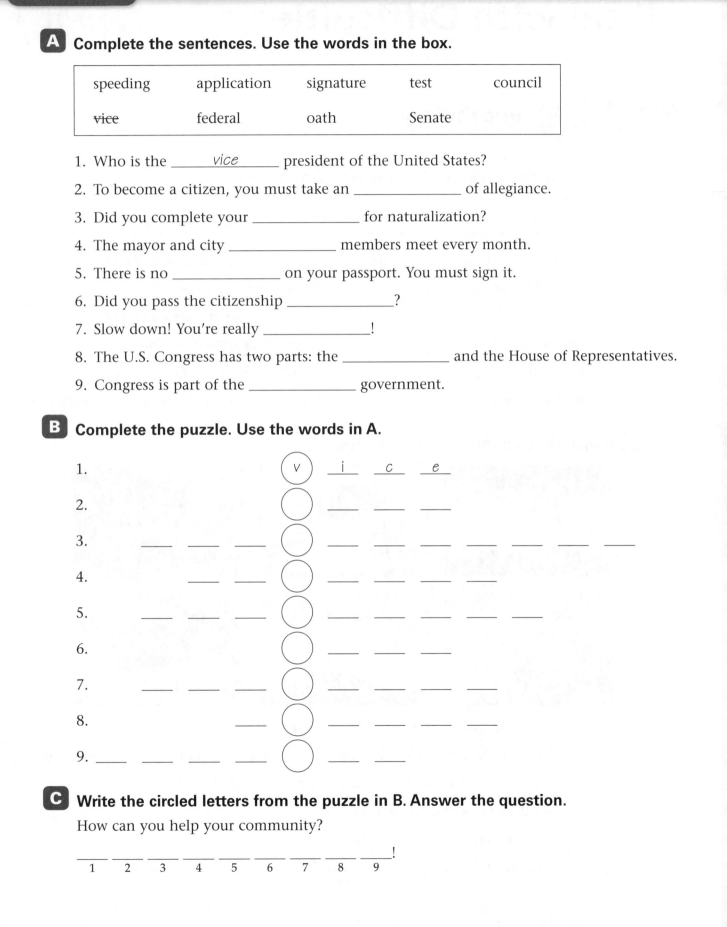

1. (v) _i_ _c_ _e_

2. ( ) ___ ___ ___

3. ___ ___ ___ ( ) ___ ___ ___ ___ ___ ___ ___ ___

4. ___ ___ ( ) ___ ___ ___

5. ___ ___ ___ ( ) ___ ___ ___ ___

6. ( ) ___ ___ ___

7. ___ ___ ___ ( ) ___ ___ ___ ___

8. ___ ( ) ___ ___ ___ ___

9. ___ ___ ___ ___ ( ) ___ ___

C **Write the circled letters from the puzzle in B. Answer the question.**

How can you help your community?

___ ___ ___ ___ ___ ___ ___ ___ ___!
 1   2   3   4   5   6   7   8   9

UNIT 11

Deal with Difficulties

LESSON 1 Vocabulary

A Complete the sentences. Use the words in the box.

| blackout | vandalism | ~~accident~~ | robbery | explosion | mugging |

1. The traffic was heavy because there was an ___accident___ on the highway.

2. You could hear the _____ at the factory from far away.

3. The _____ victim was injured. Someone hit her and took her money.

4. It was very dark. There was a _____ in the apartment building.

5. There was a _____ at the bank. The robbers stole $1,000.

6. There was some _____ in my community. There are a lot of broken windows.

B Match the pictures with the sentences.

_d_ 1. Forest fires are common in the summer.

_____ 2. In 1991, there was a volcanic eruption at Mount Pinatubo in the Philippines.

_____ 3. Hurricanes have winds of 74 miles per hour or more.

_____ 4. It's dangerous to drive in a flood.

_____ 5. You can see a tornado coming toward you.

_____ 6. After the blizzard, there were three feet of snow on the ground.

A **Rewrite the paragraph. Begin each sentence with a capital letter. End each sentence with a period. Use capital letters for names.**

steve and nancy were driving home at 8 o'clock last night on the corner of grant avenue and park street they saw an accident there was smoke coming out of the car they saw a young man in the car steve called 911 on his cell phone an ambulance and a fire truck arrived in five minutes the man in the car was not hurt

_____ _Steve and Nancy were driving home at 8 o'clock last night. On the corner of_

_____

_____

_____

_____

_____

_____

_____

_____

_____

B **Look at A. Mark the sentences T (true) or F (false).**

_F_ 1. Steve and Nancy were driving to the airport.

____ 2. There was a young man inside the car.

____ 3. Steve called 911 for help.

____ 4. One person was hurt.

C **Read the paragraph. Then complete the emergency report.**

Paul Smith and his two sons returned home yesterday and saw that something was wrong! The front door of their house at 522 Lane Avenue was open. The TV and the computer were not in the house. Paul immediately called 911 to report a robbery. They waited outside for the police.

Emergency Report
Name:_____
Place:_____
Emergency:_____

A **Read the story. Circle the correct forms of the verbs.**

Cristina and her daughter Adriana are from Peru. They usually ((visit)/ visited) their family there once a year.
₁
They (were leaving / left) for Lima last Monday. When they
₂
(arrived / were arriving) at the airport, Cristina's father and
₃
mother (waited / were waiting) for them.
₄

Cristina and Adriana always (enjoy / were enjoying)
₅
their time in Peru. On this trip, they (go / went) to the city
₆
of Cuzco and visited the famous ruins in Machu Picchu. It was a sunny day, and there
(are / were) a lot of people there. Everyone (is taking / was taking) pictures. One man
₇   ₈
(plays / was playing) a flute. The music was beautiful.
₉

Cristina and Adriana (are / were) back home now, and they are talking about their
₁₀
trip for next year!

B **Answer the questions about Cristina and Adriana. Use the information in A.**
Use complete sentences.

1. How often do Cristina and Adriana visit their family?

   They usually visit them once a year.

2. Who was waiting for them at the airport?

   _____

3. Where did they go on this trip?

   _____

4. What was everyone doing at Machu Picchu?

   _____

5. Where are Cristina and Adriana now?

   _____

C **Match the questions with the answers.**

_b_ 1. What was he doing when you arrived?   a. He took the bus.

____ 2. How did he get to work?   b. He was watching TV.

____ 3. What time do they leave?   c. We usually drive.

____ 4. How do you get to the movie theater?   d. They were sleeping.

____ 5. What were the children doing?   e. They usually leave at 6 p.m.

D **Complete the conversation. Use the simple past or past continuous of the verbs in parentheses.**

Ron: Hi Jose. I have to tell you about an emergency I _____*saw*_____
_____ yesterday. (see)

Joe: Really? What _____2_____? (happen)

Ron: Well, I _____3_____ to my car when I _____4_____
a bank robbery. (walk, see)

Joe: _____5_____ you call 911? (do)

Ron: Yes, I _____6_____ 911 immediately. (call) The operator
_____7_____ me some questions. (ask) Then she said, "The police
will be there in five minutes."

Joe: Did the police really arrive in five minutes?

Ron: Yes, they _____8_____. (do) When they _____9_____,
the robber _____10_____ away in his car. (arrive, drive)

Joe: What happened next?

Ron: I don't know. I was late for work, so I _____11_____! (leave)

E 🚀 **Grammar Boost** **Complete the sentences. Use the words in parentheses and your own information. Use the present, past, and future.**

1. (eat lunch)

   Kurt usually _eats lunch at 1:00 every day_____.

   Yesterday, _he ate lunch at 12:30_____.

   Tomorrow, _____.

2. (study English)

   I usually _____.

   Yesterday, _____.

   Tomorrow, _____.

3. (eat breakfast)

   My friends usually _____.

   Yesterday, _____.

   Tomorrow, _____.

A Complete the conversation. Use the words in the box.

2201 Beverly Hills Road	(914) 555-0602	~~the emergency~~
What happened	fire truck	

911: 911. What's _____the emergency_____?
                                    1
Mei: It's a fire emergency.

911: _____?
                    2
Mei: I left a pot on the stove.

911: What is your address?

Mei: It's _____.
                        3
911: What number are you calling from?

Mei: _____. What should I do?
                        4
911: Leave the house immediately, and wait for the _____.
                                                                        5

B Look at the graphs. Answer the questions.

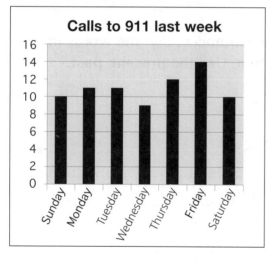

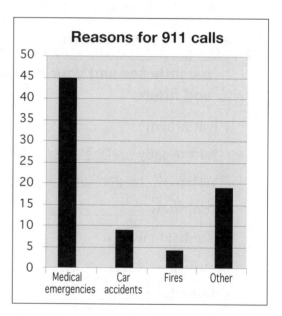

1. Which day had more calls, Friday or Saturday? _____Friday_____

2. Which day had only nine calls? _____

3. How many calls were there during the week? _____

4. How many calls were there for a medical emergency? _____

5. Which reason was more common, fires or car accidents? _____

A Read the brochure.

Protect Your Home

Do you want to make your home safe?
Here are a few things you can do to protect your home.

1. Make it difficult for strangers to come into your home. Buy good locks for your doors. A robber will often leave if it's difficult to get into your home.

2. Make sure you know your neighbors. They can call 911 for you, and you can do the same for them.

3. Have a lot of lights around your house. Use motion lights[1] outside. They help other people see robbers.

4. Get an alarm. It will make a loud sound when a robber opens your door.

Remember: Be safe and be prepared.
Call for help if you feel unsafe.

[1]**motion lights:** lights that turn on when someone moves near them

B Complete the sentences. Use words from the brochure in A.

1. You should make your house ___difficult___ to enter.

2. It's a good idea to know your _____.

3. _____ lights will help other people see robbers.

4. An _____ will make a loud sound.

5. These ideas will protect your home from a _____.

Look at the pictures. Complete the crossword puzzle.

Across

1.

9.

4.

10.

6.

12.

Down

2.

7.

3.

8.

5.

11.

1 b l i z z 2 a r d

UNIT 12

Take the Day Off

LESSON 1   Vocabulary

A   **Match the sentences with the pictures.**

1   2   3   4   5

_____   Paula likes to go biking in September.

_1_   David likes to go camping in April.

_____   Tom sometimes goes fishing in August.

_____   Lucy usually goes hiking in May.

_____   Simon always goes skating in November.

B   **Look at the pictures. Match the parts of the sentences.**

_a_   1. *The Adventure Boys* is an   a. action computer game.

_____   2. *The Longest Nightmare* is a   b. romantic movie.

_____   3. *Trip to the Stars* is a   c. horror movie.

_____   4. *Love in August* is a   d. science fiction movie.

_____   5. *The Stolen Notebook* is a   e. mystery book.

A Read the sentences. Number the sentences in the correct order. Then use the sentences to write the paragraph.

☐ On Thursday, Angela and her family are planning to go to the zoo.

[1] ~~Next weekend is a four-day weekend.~~

☐ They plan to visit the museum on Saturday afternoon.

☐ On Friday, they want to see *The Stolen Notebook*.

☐ Her children want to watch a soccer game on TV on Saturday evening.

☐ On Sunday afternoon, they are going to a concert in the park.

_____Next weekend is a four-day weekend._____

_____

_____

_____

_____

_____

_____

B Read the newspaper ad. Answer the questions.

1. When does the first show for *Lady Blue* start?

   It starts at 12:35.

2. When does the last show for *Found in Chicago* start?

   _____

3. How much is a ticket for a child under the age of 12?

   _____

4. How much is a ticket for a 66-year-old adult?

   _____

5. Alan wants to see *Lady Blue* at 3:15. He is 45 years old. How much is his ticket?

   _____

Movie Studio 400

The Stolen Notebook
1:50, 4:20, 7:50, 10:00

Found in Chicago
2:35, 5:45, 8:30

Lady Blue
12:35, 3:15, 6:20, 9:40

Children under the age of 12 – $3.50
Adults – $5.00
Seniors over 65 – $4.00

Special discount today!

$1 off all shows before 4 p.m.!

A Complete the chart. Write the correct forms of the adjectives.

Adjective	Comparative	Superlative
1. funny	funnier	the funniest
2.	sadder	
3. large		
4.		the most exciting
5.	scarier	
6.		the best
7.	worse	
8. famous		
9.		the longest
10. popular		

B Complete the questions and answers. Use the superlative of the adjectives in parentheses.

1. A: What was _____the longest_____ movie this year? (long)

   B: *Found in Chicago* _____was the longest movie this year_____.

2. A: What was _____ movie this year? (good)

   B: *Lady Blue* _____.

3. A: Who was _____ actress in the movie? (famous)

   B: Jane Smith _____.

4. A: What was _____ movie this year? (bad)

   B: *Monsters and Elephants* _____.

5. A: What was _____ movie last year? (exciting)

   B: *Darkness* _____.

6. A: What was _____ movie this year? (funny)

   B: *Clown Time* _____.

C **Read the list. Complete the questions. Then write the answers.
Use the superlative.**

1. What's ____the cheapest____ Sunday activity?

   The cheapest Sunday activity is a free concert in the park.

2. What's _____ restaurant?

   _____.

3. What's _____ movie?

   _____.

4. What's _____ museum?

   _____.

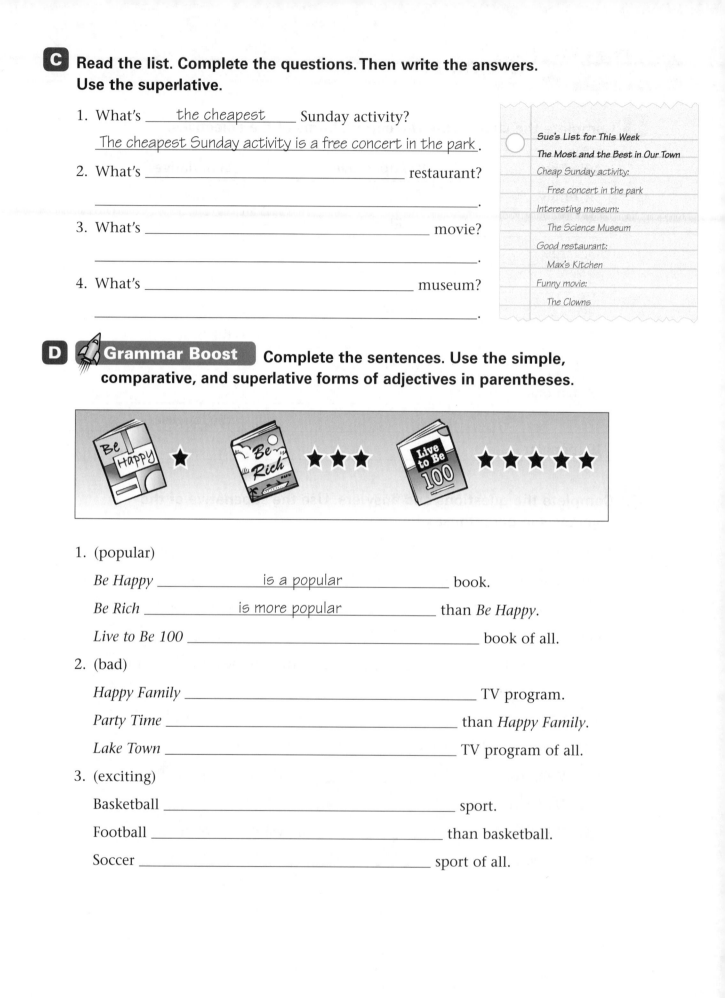

Sue's List for This Week
The Most and the Best in Our Town
Cheap Sunday activity:
    Free concert in the park
Interesting museum:
    The Science Museum
Good restaurant:
    Max's Kitchen
Funny movie:
    The Clowns

D 🚀 **Grammar Boost**   **Complete the sentences. Use the simple,
comparative, and superlative forms of adjectives in parentheses.**

1. (popular)

   Be Happy ____is a popular____ book.

   Be Rich ____is more popular____ than *Be Happy*.

   Live to Be 100 _____ book of all.

2. (bad)

   Happy Family _____ TV program.

   Party Time _____ than *Happy Family*.

   Lake Town _____ TV program of all.

3. (exciting)

   Basketball _____ sport.

   Football _____ than basketball.

   Soccer _____ sport of all.

A Complete the conversation. Use the words in the box.

most exciting	the greatest actors	~~was it~~
don't like romantic	you think of it	did you do

A: I heard you went to the basketball game last Saturday. How _____was it?_____
1

B: Great! It was the _____ game this season.
2

How about you? What _____?
3

A: My wife and I saw that new movie, *Lady Blue*.

B: Hmmm. What did _____?
4

A: Frank Davis was great. He's probably one of _____ in
5

movies today.

B: Really?

A: But I _____ movies.
6

B: Yeah, I understand.

B **Real-life math** Answer the questions.

ANNUAL COUNTY FAIR
REGULAR ADMISSION

ADULTS: $9.00   SENIORS OVER 60: $5.00
CHILDREN UNDER 12: $4.00

COME BEFORE 10 A.M.: ALL TICKETS ARE HALF PRICE!

Mr. and Mrs. Wong and their grandchildren, Kevin, Nancy, and Sue are planning to go to the County Fair this Sunday. Mr. Wong is 65, Mrs. Wong is 58, Kevin is 14, Nancy is 10, and Sue is 8 years old.

1. How much will the family spend at the County Fair for regular admission?

   _____

2. Mr. Wong says that it is too expensive, so they arrive at the fair before 10 a.m. How much do those tickets cost?

   _____

LESSON 5 · Real-life reading

A Read the online article.

Family Trip.com

TRAVEL TIPS | MAPS | WHERE TO STAY | SMART PACKING | HOME ◀ ▶

Road Trip

Family car trips are popular in the United States. They are cheaper than plane trips, and you can see much more from the car. You can visit many interesting places in a car, and the trip can be fun and exciting. Before you hit the road[1], you should be prepared. Here are some important tips before you take your next family car trip:

1. Car
Take your car to a mechanic. Ask him to check the car and make sure it is safe for the trip.

2. Maps
Get maps, guides, and travel brochures. You don't want to get lost, and it's helpful to plan your trip before you hit the road. Go to the library or look on the Internet for ideas.

3. Food and Water
Bring lots of water and healthy snacks. You might not be able to find a store or restaurant very easily.

4. Emergency road kit
Bring an emergency road kit that includes a flashlight, blankets, and a first-aid kit. Remember to be prepared before you take a family car trip. And remember to have fun!

[1] hit the road: start driving

B Answer the questions.

1. Why are family car trips popular in the United States?

   Family car trips are cheaper than plane trips, and you can see much more

   from a car.

2. What should your mechanic do before a car trip?

   _____

3. Why should you bring maps and directions?

   _____

4. Why should you bring water and snacks?

   _____

5. What should you have in your emergency road kit?

   _____

A There are over 18 words in the loop. Can you find them all? Write the words below.

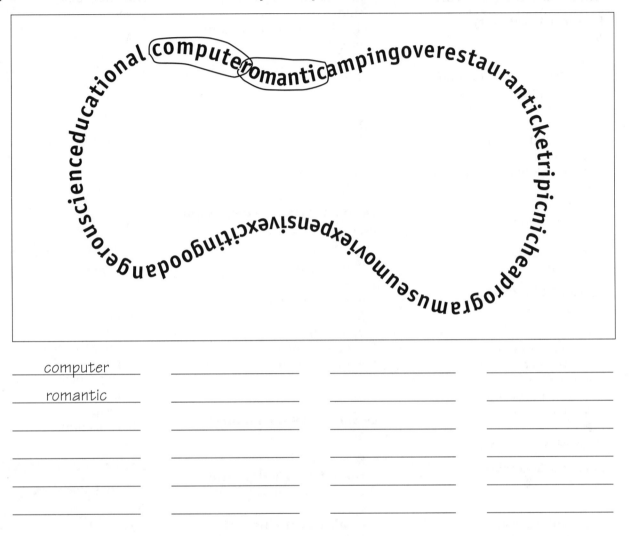

computer			
romantic			

B How many words can you make using the letters in "educational program"?
Write as many words as you can. Each word must have 3 or more letters.

educational program

late			
map			

> How many did you find?
>
> 10 words = ★ Good work!
> 15 words = ★★ Great job!
> 20+ words = ★★★ Excellent!

Unit 1 Learning to Learn

Lesson 1 Vocabulary
page 2

A

4 – David likes to look up words in the dictionary.
5 – Kalila likes to copy new words in her notebook.
3 – Dan likes to brainstorm new words.
2 – Terrell likes to listen to CDs.

B

2. pair
3. the Internet
4. group
5. flashcards
6. chart

Lesson 2 Life stories
page 3

A

2. on the Internet
3. a partner
4. listen to
5. copy new words
6. a good listener

B

Answers will vary.

Lesson 3 Grammar
page 4

A

2. wants to work
3. like to study
4. need to use
5. want to work

B

2. Yoshi doesn't like to study alone. He likes to study with a partner.
3. They don't need to study the simple past. They need to study the simple present.
4. Fernando doesn't want a math book. He wants a grammar book.

page 5

C

2. How does Brenda like to learn?

3. When do they need to study?
4. Where does she want to meet?

D

2. a
3. c
4. b

E

2. b
3. a
4. a
5. b

Lesson 4 Everyday conversation
page 6

A

2. your name
3. How do you
4. It's nice to meet

B

2. do you spell
3. do you spell
4. to meet you

C

8

Lesson 5 Real-life reading
page 7

B

Goal: Be a good parent.
2. Play with my kids every evening.
Goal: Learn a new skill.
1. Learn to use a computer.
2. Take a class in house repairs.
Goal: Save $25 every month.
1. Bring my lunch to work 3 days a week.
2. Put $5 in the bank every week.
Goal: Make new friends.
1. Go out for coffee with my classmates.
2. Have a party for my neighbors.

C

Answers will vary.

Another look
page 8

A

E	V	G	O	A	L	U	L	I	K	B	T	V
G	Y	N	U	L	I	S	T	E	N	E	R	F
U	M	I	L	O	P	T	E	W	A	Z	X	L
H	G	E	N	T	P	O	C	U	C	E	M	A
S	I	D	U	H	K	N	F	R	I	D	G	S
T	N	U	H	I	F	C	H	A	R	T	Z	H
E	Z	C	W	X	C	A	B	N	E	A	K	C
P	L	A	N	X	L	R	G	R	C	D	E	A
S	Y	T	B	X	J	S	D	E	I	F	T	R
H	B	I	J	N	T	E	U	U	P	N	V	D
E	R	O	N	X	Y	P	T	E	E	O	I	S
B	S	N	B	R	A	I	N	S	T	O	R	M
P	R	A	C	T	I	C	E	W	E	X	R	T

B

1. flashcards
2. chart
3. brainstorm
4. goal
5. steps, plan
6. listener
7. recipe
8. education

Unit 2 Getting Together

Lesson 1 Vocabulary
page 9

A

2. a
3. b
4. b
5. b

B

2. icy
3. thunderstorm
4. snowstorm
5. hot
6. freezing

Lesson 2 Life stories
page 10

A

2. beautiful fall days
3. cool and sunny
4. to go for walks
5. his vacation
6. some friends

B
2. It's on Saturday, October 14th.
3. It's on Monday, October 9th.
4. It's on Saturday, October 7th.

Lesson 3 Grammar
page 11

A
2. won't go
3. will see
4. will be
5. will visit
6. won't end

B
2. Walter won't go to his brother's graduation in March. He'll go to his brother's graduation in April.
3. Walter won't visit his parents in January. He'll visit his parents in February.
4. Walter won't go on vacation in April. He'll go on vacation in January.

C
2. c
3. d
4. b
5. a

page 12

D
2. b
3. a
4. b
5. b

E
2. Tom will talk to Mr. Diaz at work tomorrow at 8:00 a.m. tomorrow.
3. Mario will see Phil at the restaurant tomorrow at 7:00 p.m.
4. Emily won't study with Don tomorrow.

Lesson 4 Everyday conversation
page13

A
2. Go straight
3. turn right
4. the bridge
5. that's it
6. next to
7. Go up

B
b

Lesson 5 Real-life reading
page 14

B
2. b
3. a
4. a
5. b

Another look
page 15

Unit 3 Moving Out

Lesson 1 Vocabulary
page 16

A
2. mice
3. dripping faucet
4. broken door
5. leaking pipe
6. no electricity

B
2. c
3. b
4. a
5. e
6. d

Lesson 2 Life stories
page 17

A
2. five bedrooms
3. There was also
4. the big house
5. small apartment
6. very sunny
7. have two
8. for the children

B
2. T
3. T
4. F
5. F
6. F

Lesson 3 Grammar
page 18

A
3. smaller
4. prettier
5. more convenient
6. quieter
7. more expensive
8. noisier
9. larger
10. worse

B
2. Apartment 1D is more expensive than apartment 4F.
3. Apartment 1D is larger than apartment 4F.
4. Apartment 4F is cheaper than apartment 1D.
5. Apartment 4F is smaller than apartment 1D.

page 19

C
2. sunnier, the house or the cabin; Answers will vary.
3. bigger, the house or the cabin; Answers will vary.
4. prettier, the house or the cabin; Answers will vary.
5. more comfortable, the house or the cabin; Answers will vary.
6. more expensive, the house or the cabin; Answers will vary.

D
3. The apartment has a big living room, but the kitchen is very small.
4. The apartment is large, and it's near a shopping center.

Lesson 4 Everyday conversation
page 20

A
2. 2 bedrooms
3. 1st
4. security deposit
5. $350

B
2. e
3. b
4. f
5. a
6. d

C
b

Lesson 5 Real-life reading
page 21

A
Answers will vary.

C
2. Miami has a larger population than Boston.
3. Eagle has a smaller population than Wichita.
4. Boston has more expensive houses than Wichita.
5. Miami has cheaper houses than Eagle.

Another look
page 22

Household Problems
broken door, mice, no electricity

Repair People
locksmith plumber, exterminator, electrician

Rooms in a House
bedroom, living room, bathroom, kitchen

Places to Live
big city, small town, large house, sunny apartment

Unit 4 Looking for Work

Lesson 1 Vocabulary
page 23

A
2. Education
3. Employment history
4. Job skills
5. References

B
2. d
3. b
4. a

Lesson 2 Life stories
page 24

A
2. job interviews
3. on time
4. clean and neat
5. a suit and tie
6. the interviewer
7. make eye contact
8. be nervous

B
2. part-time
3. experience, required

4. references
5. immediately

Lesson 3 Grammar,
page 25

A
2. talked
3. got
4. went
5. applied
6. wrote

B
2. had, She didn't have a job interview at the bank.
3. worked, He didn't work at Roy's Supermarket.
4. got, She didn't get a job at the post office.
5. filled out, He didn't fill out a job application for a job at the library.
6. read, I didn't read the newspaper.

page 26

C
2. A: Did Keisha work at State Bank for ten years? B: No, she didn't.
3. A: Did Gao graduate from the University of Pennsylvania? B: No, he didn't.
4. A: Did Gao work at Lewis Elementary School for three years? B: No, he didn't.

D
Possible answers are:
She's a cashier at the store on the corner.
He was good at languages.
He was a cashier at the store on the corner.
They have experience using computers.
They got their GEDs last year.
We have experience using computers.

Lesson 4 Everyday conversation
page 27

B
2. computer science
3. two years
4. office manager
5. computers
6. with people
7. Carla Santiago

C
2. He worked as a computer programmer at BZD, Inc. for four and a half years.

Lesson 5 Real-life reading
page 28

B
2. a
3. b
4. a
5. b

Another look
page 29

JOB APPLICATION			

Personal Infomation

NAME (LAST/FIRST)			
Wilson, Kate			

ADDRESS (NUMBER/STREET)	(CITY)		(CITY/STATE)
2121 Post Street	Denver		Colorado

TELEPHONE (DAY)	(EVENING)		
(303) 555-6520	303-555-7750		

EMAIL			
kate@internet.us			

Employment History (Start with most recent job)

EMPLOYER 1 (NAME)	(POSITION)	(DATES)	(CITY/STATE)
Simm's Restaurant	Service Manager	2004-present	Denver, Colorado
EMPLOYER 2 (NAME)	(POSITION)	(DATES)	(CITY/STATE)
Flynn's Restaurant	Asst. Manager	2002–2004	Denver, Colorado

Education (Start with most recent)

SCHOOL 1 (NAME)	(DEGREE)	(DATES)	(CITY/STATE)
State University	bachelor's degree	2000-2002	Denver, Colorado
SCHOOL 2 (NAME)	(DEGREE)	(DATES)	(CITY/STATE)
City Community College	associate's degree	1998-2000	Denver, Colorado

Job Skills

COMPUTER SKILLS	LANGUAGES		
☑ YES ☐ NO	English, Spanish		

Reference

NAME	RELATION/CONTACT		PHONE #
Jennifer Long	Employer		(303) 555-2134

Unit 5 On the Job

Lesson 1 Vocabulary
page 30

A
Kinds of pay
net pay
Deductions
Social Security, federal tax
Earnings
hourly rate, pay period

B
The following items should be checked:
computer
photocopier
file cabinet
vending machine
fax machine

C
2. computer
3. fax machine
4. photocopier

Lesson 2 Life stories
page 31

A
2. on time
3. a uniform
4. needs to
5. time clock
6. pay period
7. the deductions
8. net pay

B
2. Both
3. Both
4. School
5. Work
6. Both

Lesson 3 Grammar
page 32

A
2. She might get a raise. She might not get a raise.
3. I might be late for work. I might not be late for work.
4. They might make a mistake. They might not make a mistake.

B
2. might go
3. might get
4. might get
5. might not finish
6. might help

page 33

C
Things Linda should do
She should shake hands.
She should ask questions.
Things Linda shouldn't do
She shouldn't be late.
She shouldn't be nervous.

D
2. have to
3. might
4. shouldn't
5. might
6. might not

Lesson 4 Everyday conversation
page 34

A
2. right away
3. that letter
4. scan these
5. make copies
6. use the forklift

B
2. Could you type this letter, please?
3. Could you help me with my computer please?

Lesson 5 Real-life reading
page 35

B
2. ✓ Doesn't complain about little things.
3. ✓ Wants to learn new things
4. ✓ Is a hard worker
5. ✓ Follows important rules
6. ✓ Is on time for work

Another look
page 36

A
fax machine – P
printer – F
scanner – F
photocopier – P
window – B
time clock – B
safety glasses – P
file cabinet – B

B
2. computer
3. printer
4. safety glasses
5. fax machine
6. computer

Unit 5 Pick Up the Phone

Lesson 1 Vocabulary
page 37

A
2. $24.00
3. Domestic, International
4. $52.50

B
2. pay phone, a taxi
3. cell phone, emergency services
4. answering machine, a message

Lesson 2 Life stories
page 38

A
2. sick child
3. a bad cold
4. had to stay
5. is angry
6. to get fired

B
2. My child has a fever.
3. I'm tired today.
4. I feel terrible. I have a cold.

Lesson 3 Grammar
page 39

A
Answers will vary.

B
2. were eating lunch
3. was jogging
4. were studying
5. was making dinner
6. was reading his email

C
Answers will vary.

page 40

D
2. they weren't making coffee
3. he wasn't working
4. I was exercising

E
2. b
3. a
4. f
5. e
6. d

F
3. is studying
4. Was, driving
5. are taking
6. was, doing
7. am eating
8. were, going

Lesson 4 Everyday conversation
page 41

A
2. speak to Mr. Gonzalez
3. isn't in
4. May I take
5. This is
6. give him the message

B
For: Mr. Gonzalez
From: Carlos Hernandez
Message: Please call Carlos. His phone number is 555-4724.

C
b

Lesson 5 Real-life reading
page 42

B
2. F
3. F

Another look
page 43

A
2. cell phone
3. local service
4. make a call
5. total due
B
He is making a long distance call.

Unit 7 What's for Dinner?

Lesson 1 Vocabulary
page 44

A
2. can
3. bunch
4. bottle
5. box
6. jar
7. bag
8. carton
B
2. jar
3. bottle
4. can
5. bunch
6. carton

Lesson 2 Life stories
page 45

A
2. supermarket advertisements
3. prices
4. unit prices
5. a lot of coupons
6. at saving money
7. a problem
8. cheap
B
2. Five ounces for $1.90 is a better buy.
3. One pint for $2.75 is a better buy.
4. Two bunches for $2.99 is a better buy.

Lesson 3 Grammar
page 46

A
count nouns: potatoes, mushrooms
noncount nouns: salt, water

B
2. check How much, How much soda;
3. check How much, How much flour;
4. check How many, How many bananas
C
2. How many
3. How many
4. How much

page 47

D
2. She doesn't have any tomatoes.
3. There's some salt in the soup.
4. He doesn't eat any cheese.
5. We want some oil.
E
1. B: a; A: some
2. A: an, some; B: How many, some; A: any
3. A: How much; B: any; A: some
4. A: any; B: How many

Lesson 4 Everyday conversation
page 48

A
2. Clerk: The tuna is in aisle. next to the soup.
3. Keiko: OK, aisle 3. Thank you. Oh, and the sausages?
4. Clerk: Sausages? You can find them in the meat section.
5. Keiko: That's everything I need. Thanks a lot.
6. Clerk: You're welcome.
B
baked goods – 3
dairy – 4
meat – 2
canned goods – 5
C
a

Lesson 5 Real-life reading
page 49

B
2. F – Yogurt has calcium.
3. T
4. F – Potato chips aren't healthier than nuts.
5. T

C
2. How much is one serving?
3. How many calories are in one serving?
4. How many calories from fat are in one serving?

Another look
page 50

A

B	U	N	C	H	Y	J	N	H	P	I	N	T
W	E	J	N	V	U	T	R	O	Y	Q	Z	M
S	X	Z	V	F	A	W	A	U	Q	B	A	G
N	N	S	K	J	U	I	S	N	B	T	D	W
C	N	L	K	U	P	A	T	C	O	G	E	Q
P	A	C	K	A	G	E	O	E	F	H	K	U
R	J	A	H	Y	Z	M	Q	S	H	Y	D	A
T	V	R	T	E	I	I	T	M	W	N	X	R
O	P	T	Y	U	V	Z	N	N	O	M	Y	T
N	N	O	R	E	V	O	Z	N	D	W	C	T
C	W	N	A	P	O	U	N	D	W	X	A	Y
A	S	B	B	L	R	D	N	T	X	Z	N	T
J	N	A	Q	M	S	S	B	O	X	X	Y	Y

B
Meat: a pound of sausages
Dairy: A pint of ice cream, a carton of milk
Drinks: a quart of juice, a can of soda
Produce: a bunch of bananas, a bag of apples
Baked goods: a box of cookies, a package of bread

Unit 8 Stay Safe and Well

Lesson 1 Vocabulary
page 51

A
2. antihistamine
3. pain reliever
4. antacid
5. eardrops
6. antibiotic ointment
B
3 - Alex has a rash.
2 - Midori is sneezing and has a runny nose.
4 - Carlos has a fever.
6 - Lisa is nauseus and dizzy.
5 - Julie has a cough.

Lesson 2 Life stories
page 52

A
2. made an appointment
3. gave him a filling
4. had a backache
5. to the chiropractor
6. have to rest

B
2. see the pediatrician
3. the problem
4. about 11:30
5. Could you make
6. That's good

Lesson 3 Grammar
page 53

A
2. was playing, broke
3. were watching, got
4. was reading, hurt
5. were having, arrived
6. was cooking, cut

B
2. The children were playing soccer when they saw an accident.
3. Binita was studying when she got a headache.
4. Natasha and Boris were skiing when they fell in love.
5. He was cleaning when he hurt his back.

C
Answers will vary.

page 54

D
1. B: was cooking
2. B: had an, was painting
3. B: his arm, was playing

E
2. they leave
3. she drive
4. were you watching
5. he hurt

Lesson 4 Everyday conversation
page 55

A
2. How often
3. times a day
4. take more than
5. for ten days
6. refill the prescription

B
2. T
3. T
4. F
5. F

C
1. a
2. a

Lesson 5 Real-life reading
page 56

B
2. F
3. T
4. T
5. F

C
Check: scissors, gloves, antiseptic wipes

Another look
page 57

A
3-down: bandage
2-down: runny
9-across: sneezing
6-across: allergic
4-across: antihistamine
8-across: fever
1-down: pain
5-down: injured
7-across: swollen

B

Unit 9 Money Matters

Lesson 1 Vocabulary
page 58

A
2. current balance
3. personal check
4. ATM card
5. savings account
6. credit card bill

B
2. your PIN
3. insert the deposit
4. enter the amount
5. take your cash
6. remove your

Lesson 2 Life stories
page 59

A
2. makes a list
3. a picnic table
4. total budget
5. compare the prices
6. has a special offer
7. a great bargain
8. cost $35
9. he goes home
10. have picnics

B
computer desk: $80
comfortable chair: $65
picture for the wall: $55

Lesson 3 Grammar
page 60

A
2. c
3. a
4. b

B
2. it
3. they
4. X
5. it
6. they

C
2. He went to the bank to deposit a check.
3. She went to the library to return some books.
4. He went to the ATM because he needed some cash.
5. He went to the baseball game because he had tickets.
6. They went to the supermarket because they wanted some sugar.

page 61

D
2. to withdraw some cash
3. to refill a prescription
4. wanted some books

E
Answers will vary.

Lesson 4 Everyday conversation
page 62

A

2. Clerk: OK. Why are you returning it?
3. Customer: Because it's too big. I need a smaller one. Here's my receipt.
4. Clerk: Would you like a refund, or do you want to exchange the shirt?
5. Customer: I'd like to exchange it, please.

B

2. Why are you returning it?
3. Because I don't like the color.
4. I don't have it.
5. You can't get a refund without a receipt.
6. I'll exchange it for a different color.

C

a

Lesson 5 Real-life reading
page 63

B

2. You should call the credit card company immediately.
3. You should send a letter to the credit card company.
4. You should look at your next credit card bill carefully.
5. You should keep the credit card company's phone number in a safe place.

Another look
page 64

A

D	E	P	O	S	I	T	F	C	A	B	C	O	R	H
T	Z	H	P	A	W	N	E	N	U	G	W	D	B	M
I	N	M	C	X	L	B	E	R	E	T	U	R	N	P
V	Y	U	R	G	H	U	M	Q	A	R	D	O	S	K
U	K	X	E	B	N	D	E	C	M	R	V	V	S	L
P	T	M	D	C	I	G	T	X	C	H	E	C	K	D
Q	D	E	I	E	C	E	A	C	L	S	K	R	B	T
U	C	E	T	B	O	T	A	T	J	I	F	E	P	L
P	S	K	C	O	U	I	S	O	M	X	G	B	W	D
M	P	B	A	N	K	S	T	A	T	E	M	E	N	T
L	V	C	R	E	H	D	N	J	N	H	K	Q	J	D
W	D	F	D	I	F	B	A	W	O	I	P	N	E	M
R	Y	M	B	H	N	D	J	Y	F	H	T	P	S	X
S	A	V	I	N	G	S	A	C	C	O	U	N	T	U
B	A	L	A	N	C	E	W	R	K	A	N	A	X	Y

B

2. savings account
3. return
4. deposit
5. credit card
6. bank statement
7. check
8. budget

Unit 10 Steps to Citizenship

Lesson 1 Vocabulary
page 65

A

4 - take the oath of allegiance
3 - take a citizenship test
5 - get a passport
2 - fill out an application for naturalization

B

Federal Government
U.S. senator, vice president, U.S. representative, president

State Government
governor, lieutenant governor

Local Government
city council members, mayor

Lesson 2 Life stories
page 66

A

2. people at the meeting
3. Grant Park is dirty
4. doesn't have enough
5. had an idea
6. decided to do
7. to raise money
8. help clean the park

B

2. The date for the park clean up is June 17th.
3. It starts at 10:00 a.m.
4. No, they don't.
5. Call Angela Banks for more information.

Lesson 3 Grammar
page 67

A

2. must not
3. must not
4. must
5. must not
6. must

B

2. T
3. F   You must arrive on time.
4. T
5. F   You must not put your feet in the aisle.

page 68

C

2. must not, must
3. must not, must
4. must, must not

D

2. shouldn't
3. must not
4. must not
5. Can
6. can
7. should
8. might not

Lesson 4 Everyday conversation
page 69

A

2. I see
3. photo ID
4. it is
5. photo is
6. take care of it

B

2. a
3. c
4. b
5. d

C

2. must not
3. must
4. should

Lesson 5 Real-life reading
page 70

B

2. F
3. F
4. F
5. T
6. F

Another look
page 71

A

2. oath
3. application
4. council
5. signature
6. test
7. speeding
8. Senate
9. federal

B

2. oath
3. application

4. council
5. signature
6. test
7. speeding
8. Senate
9. federal
C
volunteer

Unit 11 Deal with Difficulties

Lesson 1 Vocabulary
page 72

A
2. explosion
3. mugging
4. blackout
5. robbery
6. vandalism
B
2. e
3. b
4. c
5. a
6. f

Lesson 2 Life stories
page 73

A
  Steve and Nancy were driving home at 8 o'clock last night. On the corner of Grant Avenue and Park Street, they saw an accident. There was smoke coming out of the car. They saw a young man in the car. Steve called 911 on his cell phone. An ambulance and a fire truck arrived in five minutes. The man in the car was not hurt.
B
2. T
3. T
4. F
C
Name: Paul Smith
Place: 522 Lane Avenue
Emergency: robbery

Lesson 3 Grammar
page 74

A
2. left
3. arrived

4. were waiting
5. enjoy
6. went
7. were
8. was taking
9. was playing
10. are
B
2. Christina's mother and father were waiting for them.
3. They went to Peru.
4. Everyone was taking pictures.
5. They are back home now.
C
2. a
3. e
4. c
5. d

page 75

D
2. happened
3. was walking
4. saw
5. Did
6. called
7. asked
8. did
9. arrived
10. drove *or* was driving
11. left
E
Answers will vary.

Lesson 4 Everyday conversation
page 76

A
2. What happened
3. 2201 Beverly Hills Road
4. (914) 555-0602
5. fire truck
B
2. Wednesday
3. 77
4. 45
5. car accidents

Lesson 5 Real-life reading
page 77

B
2. neighbors
3. Motion
4. alarm
5. a robber *or* robbery

Another look
page 78

Unit 12 Take the Day Off

Lesson 1 Vocabulary
page 79

A
4 - Paula likes to go biking in September.
3 - Tom sometimes goes fishing in August.
2 - Lucy usually goes hiking in May.
5 - Simon always goes skating in November.
B
2. c
3. d
4. b
5. e

Lesson 2 Life stories
page 80

A
2. On Thursday, Angela and her family are planning to go to the zoo.
4. They plan to visit the museum on Saturday afternoon.
3. On Friday, they want to see *The Stolen Notebook*.
5. Her children want to watch a soccer game on TV on Saturday evening.
6. On Sunday afternoon, they are going to a concert in the park.

Next weekend is a four-day weekend. On Thursday, Angela and her family are planning to go to the zoo. On Friday, they want to see *The Stolen Notebook*. They plan to visit the museum on Saturday afternoon. Her children want to watch a soccer game on TV on Saturday evening. On Sunday afternoon, they are going to a concert in the park.

B
2. It starts at 8:30.
3. It's $3.50.
4. It's $4.00.
5. It's $5.00.

Lesson 3 Grammar
page 81

A
2. sad, the saddest
3. larger, the largest
4. exciting, more exciting
5. scary, the scariest
6. good, better
7. bad, the worst
8. more famous, the most famous
9. long, longer
10. more popular, the most popular

B
2. A: the best; B: was the best movie this year
3. A: the most famous; B: was the most famous actress in the movie
4. A: the worst movie of this year; B: was the worst movie this year
5. A: the most exciting; B: was the most exciting movie last year
6. A: the funniest; B: was the funniest movie this year

page 82

C
2. the best; Max's Kitchen is the best restaurant.
3. the funniest; The Clowns is the funniest movie.
4. the most interesting; The Science Museum is the most interesting museum.

D
1. is the most popular
2. is a bad, is worse, is the worst
3. is an exciting, is more exciting, is the most exciting

Lesson 4 Everyday conversation
page 83

A
2. most exciting
3. did you do
4. you think of it
5. the greatest actors
6. don't like romantic

B
1. $31.00
2. $15.50

Lesson 5 Real-life reading
page 84

B
2. The mechanic should check the car and make sure it I safe for the trip.
3. You don't want to get lost.
4. You might not be able to find a store or a restaurant very easily.
5. You should have a flashlight, blankets, and a first-aid kit in your emergency road kit.

Another look
page 85

A
Possible answers:
camping
go
over
restaurant
ticket
trip
picnic
cheap
program
museum
movie
expensive
exciting
good
dangerous
science
educational

B
Possible answers:

cat
date
deal
dog
duct
goal
goat
groan
lamp
land
late
lead
loan
mop
not
pan
plan
point
pool
ramp
run
tin
ton